Selected Poems

JOHN MASEFIELD was born in Ledbury, Herefordshire, in 1878. He was orphaned at an early age and, after a brief period at the King's School, Warwick, was educated aboard the Liverpool school-ship *Conway*. As an apprentice, Masefield sailed round Cape Horn in 1894; as a result of sickness, he was classified a Distressed British Sailor upon arrival in Chile. After convalescence in England he secured a new position in New York. Although he crossed the Atlantic, he never reported for duty. He later noted, 'I was going to be a writer, come what might.' After a period of homeless vagrancy, bar and factory work in America, Masefield returned to England in 1897. His first published poem appeared in a periodical in 1899. The friendship of W.B. Yeats provided encouragement, and in 1902 *Salt-Water Ballads* was published. A distinguished literary career followed, with work across a broad range of genres. Masefield was appointed Poet Laureate in 1930, and awarded the Order of Merit in 1935. He died in 1967; his ashes are buried in Poets' Corner, Westminster Abbey.

PHILIP W. ERRINGTON is an expert within the Department of Printed Books and Manuscripts at Sotheby's in London. A graduate of the University of London, he read for his BA, MA and PhD at University College. In 2000 he was appointed a visiting research fellow of the University of London, Institute of English Studies. He has published in the *Yeats Annual* and was appointed editor of *The Journal of the John Masefield Society* in 1997. He was responsible for, and introduced, facsimile centenary editions of Masefield's *Salt-Water Ballads* in 2002 and *Ballads* in 2003. His bibliograph of *English Literature*, was published

Fyfield*Books* aim to make available some of the great classics of British and European literature in clear, affordable formats, and to restore often neglected writers to their place in literary tradition.

Fyfield*Books* take their name from the Fyfield elm in Matthew Arnold's 'Scholar Gypsy' and 'Thyrsis'. The tree stood not far from the village where the series was originally devised in 1971.

> *Roam on! The light we sought is shining still.*
> *Dost thou ask proof? Our tree yet crowns the hill,*
> *Our Scholar travels yet the loved hill-side*

from 'Thyrsis'

JOHN MASEFIELD

Sea-Fever

Selected Poems

Edited with an introduction by
PHILIP W. ERRINGTON

Fyfield*Books*

CARCANET

I dedicate my share of this book to the memory of
J.N.E., E.F.E., J.A.O'D. and M.B.O'D.

First published in Great Britain in 2005 by
Carcanet Press Limited
Alliance House
Cross Street
Manchester M2 7AQ

The publisher acknowledges financial assistance from Arts Council England

Typeset by XL Publishing Services, Tiverton
Printed and bound in England by SRP Ltd, Exeter

Contents

1911–1921

ix

Miscellaneous Verse, 1930–1967

Introduction

John Masefield was one of the most successful, prolific, popular and long-lived writers of the twentieth century. W.B. Yeats told him 'You'll be a popular poet – you'll be riding in your carriage and pass me in the gutter',[1] and although Yeats was wrong about his own reputation he accurately identified a number of aspects about a youthful Masefield.

Masefield's early contemporary public were to buy his novels, plays, children's books, histories and poetry in huge numbers. His financial position, resulting from popularity, would not have prompted the writer to choose Yeats' extravagant mode of transport, however. Masefield's first book had opened with an emphatic rejection of 'princes and prelates with periwigged charioteers' and Masefield's poetic manifesto clearly states that he will write of 'the dirt and the dross, the dust and scum of the earth!'

Masefield was born on 1 June 1878 in Ledbury, Herefordshire.[2] His early childhood was idyllic, and the beauty of the local countryside, together with a dreamy imagination, led to a quasi-Wordsworthian communion with Nature. This 'paradise'[3] was not to last: Masefield was orphaned and entrusted to the guardianship of an aunt and uncle. His guardians hoped that training for the merchant marine would dispel aspirations to become a writer, and between 1891 and 1894 Masefield was educated aboard the Mersey school-ship *Conway*. In Liverpool, sight of the *Wanderer*, a four-masted barque, was a profound experience: it was to be a recurrent symbol throughout his work. As an apprentice, Masefield sailed round Cape Horn in 1894, but became violently ill. Classified a Distressed British Sailor he returned to England. A new position was secured for the youth aboard a ship in New York but although Masefield crossed the Atlantic he failed to report for duty. He later noted 'I deserted my ship in New York... and cut myself adrift from her, and from my home. I was going to be a writer, come what might.'[4] Homeless vagrancy ensued and became the basis for a lifelong sympathy with the underdog. Eventually, bar and factory work ended in 1897 when Masefield returned to England and started work in London as a bank clerk. Plagued by ill-health, the would-be poet achieved success in 1899 with the publication of his first poem in *The Outlook*.[5]

Masefield saw himself as a writer – rather than solely a poet – but viewing his poetic output in four chronological periods allows features of his career to become apparent.

*　*　*　*

It is during the period 1899–1911 that Masefield developed his individual voice, aided by the criticism of a close group of contemporaries. In 1900 he approached W.B. Yeats and was invited to join the circle that included Lady Gregory, Arthur Symons, J.M. Synge, Laurence Binyon and Jack B. Yeats. *Salt-Water Ballads* (1902) was Masefield's first volume, comprising over fifty, predominantly maritime, poems (including 'Sea-Fever'). The diction was intended to be idiomatic and a little shocking. Masefield himself considered the volume 'something new said newly'.[6] *Ballads* (1903) revealed a more pastoral and lyrical side to the poet, but verse was becoming increasingly difficult for the writer. In the mid-1900s Masefield even admitted to Janet Ashbee that he no longer wrote verse. Seeking financial stability, he turned away from poetry. Short stories, naval histories, drama and novels were experiments that Masefield would, later, largely disown. In 1910 *Ballads and Poems* relied on his earlier two volumes of poetry for the contents. Masefield later described the period as 'a very real blackness of despair' and noted, 'my work was not what I had hoped'.[7] This period was, however, when Masefield wrote some of his best-known, and well-loved verse.

It was in 1911, with the publication of *The Everlasting Mercy*, that Masefield arrived on the literary scene with a new and shocking voice. This long narrative poem concerning the spiritual enlightenment of a drunken poacher caused a sensation. Lord Alfred Douglas branded the work 'nine tenths sheer filth', J.M. Barrie described it as 'incomparably the finest literature'; it was denounced from the pulpit and read in public houses.[8] Masefield had found his *oeuvre* for the moment. He continued his success with *The Widow in the Bye Street* in 1912 and *Dauber* in 1914. The first comprises a rural tragedy in which lust provokes murder; the second tells of an aspiring artist's experiences at sea, during which the main character receives contempt from his fellow sailors but falls to his death after an act of heroism.

With the outbreak of war, Masefield became an orderly at a Red Cross hospital in France. Here he experienced the horror of modern warfare. He also took charge of a motor-boat ambulance service at Gallipoli in 1915 and undertook a propaganda tour of the United States. His prose work *Gallipoli* led to an invitation from Sir Douglas Haig to chronicle the battle of the Somme, although Whitehall bureaucracy eventually forced Masefield to abandon the plan. The period ends with a final flurry of long narrative poems including *Reynard the Fox* (the tale of a fox-hunt), *Right Royal* (concerning a steeple-chase) and *King Cole* (in which a travelling circus is saved from disaster by the mythological king).

In 1922 Masefield abandoned the genre of the long narrative poem and turned, once more, to novels and drama. Now living outside Oxford, he organised amateur theatrical productions and recitations. A private theatre in his garden provided a forum in which poets could develop their work. Masefield himself turned to Arthurian legend as a source for poetry. The period from 1922 to 1930 is closely associated with Masefield developing poetry as a spoken art form. The experiments in verse-speaking led to the establishment of the Oxford Recitations and later the Oxford Summer Diversions. The latter would find Masefield persuading J.R.R. Tolkien to dress up as Chaucer and recite middle English.[9] With the death of Robert Bridges, the position of Poet Laureate fell vacant and in 1930 Masefield was appointed, after recommendation by Britain's first Labour Prime Minister, Ramsay MacDonald.

The years from 1930 to 1967 comprise the longest period in my chronological sequence and represent Masefield as the fourteenth Laureate after Dryden. He continued to produce poetic work in the 1930s and early 1940s although he largely concentrated on his narrative skills in a succession of successful novels (*The Bird of Dawning* and the *Ned* trilogy, for example). The 1940s saw the Laureate turning to his love of the English countryside for inspiration (and also collaborating on a series of works with the artist Edward Seago).[10] Masefield produced a sizable quantity of 'official verse' as Laureate, for which he has frequently been attacked. Selection allows us to discard some dutiful royal verse and reclaim a number of moving and striking examples. The selection here provides – for the first time – evidence of Masefield as a war poet. 'August, 1914' is incorrectly considered Masefield's only poem on war. Verse from *The Nine Days Wonder* and *A Generation Risen* finds, however, the Georgian poet considering the Second World War, having experienced the horrors of the First. Laureateship verse published in periodicals, or contributed to other works, presents several notable examples (including 'Now' on the subject of D-Day). Other Laureateship work presented here commemorates the birth of Prince Charles ('A Hope for the Newly-Born'), and the deaths of T.S. Eliot ('East Coker') and Churchill. The story – now popular – that Masefield's humility prompted him to send Laureateship verse to *The Times* accompanied by a stamped addressed envelope in case of rejection is thought to be untrue.[11]

Serious illness struck Masefield in 1949 and the 1950s saw little published work. The final years of his life saw a resurgence of activity and success, however. Masefield died on 12 May 1967 and his ashes were interred in Poets' Corner, Westminster Abbey. In a memorial address Robert Graves stated that in Masefield 'the fierce flame of poetry had truly burned'.[12]

The four periods 1899–1911, 1911–22, 1922–30 and 1930–67 provide convenient compartments in the writer's career. I have grouped published work in chronological sequence of issue within these periods, with a final section of miscellaneous verse in each case for work that appeared in periodicals, or as contributions to other publications. This section also includes a number of rarities. Given the importance, here, of context, the source of each poem is provided within the main body of the book.

* * * *

Masefield's thematic concerns commence with the sea and, usually, the brutality of the sea. 'Sea-Fever' and 'Cargoes', in describing the lure of the sea and the rich variety of the naval heritage, are unrepresentative of Masefield's largely ambivalent views. Death is a constant threat and early verse shows a preoccupation with fever, disaster and the brutality of naval life. This is revisited in *Dauber*. There is also a spiritual side to the sea, frequently represented by the image of the *Wanderer*. This ship becomes, for Masefield, the symbol of success in failure and therefore, of course, a manifestation of the writer's sympathy for the underdog. The despised and rejected are ever-present (and would even reveal a metamorphosis into the unknown ballet dancers of 'Not Only the Most Famous'). The closing stanzas of 'The *Wanderer*' find the return of the ship heralding Christmas day. The 'defeated thing' promises regeneration. For Masefield the symbol of hope, regeneration and salvation is the crowing of a cock. Marcellus' statement in the first scene of *Hamlet* is behind Masefield's byre cock that heralds the morning and return of the *Wanderer*.

In contrast to the brutality of the sea is Masefield's sense of fun and romance. His close friendship with Jack B. Yeats is of importance here. The two men enjoyed sailing toy boats (see 'The Gara Brook' and 'The Pirate Poet on the *Monte*') and both developed a passion for tales of piracy. Coupled with an interest in traditional shanties, this led to the nonsense 'Theodore' verse. Theodore, the pirate cabin-boy, who is secretly in love with the beautiful Constanza, became a focus within private correspondence and occasional pieces for *A Broadsheet* and *A Broadside*. In 1911 Masefield admitted to Jack B. Yeats that his anthology *A Sailor's Garland* was 'full of traps' to catch '...ruffians [who] used to take the anthologies collected by other men's labour and sort them up differently and print them as their own...' Masefield then notes that in 'The Whale' he 'restored some quite unintelligible lines' and that 'The Salcombe Seaman's Flaunt to the Proud Pirate' was entirely by him.[13] 'Theodore To His Grandson', 'Die We Must' and 'The Gara River' were originally signed with the pseudonym 'Wolfe T. MacGowan'. This name has, at various times, been attributed to Jack B. Yeats. Evidence suggests, however, that these verses are Masefield's and it is therefore a pleasure to claim them for this present selection.[14]

Other Masefield concerns include the traditional opposition of town versus country, a sense of comradeship and the value of community, the presence of the 'other-worldly' (either as supernatural spirits or fairies) and the English countryside and way of life. His love of the past is manifest in Masefield's interest in the legends of Arthur, Troy and the Romans, but his themes also encompass the progress made by man against poverty. The sonnets, in particular, explore his preoccupation with natural and spiritual beauty and reawakening.

Masefield's stylistic range includes colloquial diction as well as the more 'traditional' and 'literary'. He was rarely innovative in his use of verse forms, and the sonnets, in particular, reveal a heavy reliance on Shakespeare. Yet there are numerous effects achieved by the slight manipulation of verse form through enjambment and the occasional variation of rhythmical lines that are masterly. Masefield's natural tendency is away from concise description, and he revels in the expansiveness of descriptive detail.

*   *   *   *

The task of selection has been informed by Masefield's own practice. In 1922 he published a volume of *Selected Poems* (enlarged in 1938). An entirely new edition was published in 1950. With the exception of a few long poems, this current volume includes those poems that were selected by Masefield on both occasions. Masefield's practice was to present excerpts from the long narrative poems, and I have chosen to repeat this method here. A volume of selections from both poetry and prose, entitled *A Book of Both Sorts*, was published in 1947. This, together with a small number of commercial sound-recordings, assists in identifying the author's personal favourites. I have mostly only changed text to provide editorial consistency within the edition (consistent use of single or double inverted commas, for example). All titles are authorial unless placed in square brackets. The cover illustration is by Masefield's contemporary, the artist Kenneth Shoesmith, a former *Conway* boy and well-known for his illustrations of ships. At Masefield's request he provided work for several of his books.

My copy-texts have been largely English first editions. Masefield would occasionally rework his poetry. Hence the earlier version, for example, of

'Sea-Fever' (lacking 'go' in the opening line) and a few unfamiliar readings within 'Spanish Waters'.[15] I have silently corrected a number of obvious errors and supplied a revised version of one line in 'London Town'. For texts from later in the poet's career there were numerous simultaneous English and American editions. I have opted for the English edition in such cases, for it seems that the author would allow an early proof setting of text to be sent for American publication and he may have had greater control over the English edition.[16]

* * * *

The most recent bibliography of books and pamphlets by Masefield lists 178 individual titles.[17] These, largely excluding collected or selected works, include approximately 62 differently titled volumes of poetry, 29 lectures, speeches or works of literary criticism, 17 novels, 23 plays, 10 historical works and 7 volumes for children. Masefield's poetry was respected by Thomas Hardy and Philip Larkin.[18] His plays were praised by Bernard Shaw and his novels by Graham Greene.[19] But the writer's status was to change. Masefield was first read by the Victorians and witnessed the coming of the railways at the border of his childhood garden. He also marked the assassination of J.F. Kennedy in one of his most memorable Laureateship verses. Times changed but Masefield did not change with them. In 1957 he observed that from three hundred million readers of English, three read his work and four criticised it.[20] In 1978 John Betjeman noted that 'Sea-Fever' and 'Cargoes' would be 'remembered as long as the language lasts' but even this claim on posterity demonstrates the reduction of Masefield's canon to a mere six stanzas.[21] This new *Selected Poems* presents examples of the writer's work to those for whom six stanzas is too reductive in scope.

It is all too easy to dismiss Masefield's work; today there is a critical acceptance of this perspective. John Bayley, reviewing an edition of W.H. Davies' *Selected Poems* noted that:

> Poetically speaking... Masefield had a tendency to pluck defeat from the jaws of victory, to assault the reader of the time with a formidable display of starkness and directness which has ended up seeming arty and genteel. Georgian poetry was always trying to be brutally realistic and down to earth, but never was so very convincingly.[22]

Neil Corcoran, in his review of Donald Stanford's edition of Masefield's *Selected Poems*, repeated Bayley's attack and noted:

This is witty and cruel, but it is the kind of argument which should be engaged by any editor seriously recommending Masefield to contemporary readers... Masefield sounds impressive only if you do not come too close: not as close, certainly, as Modernism and the New Criticism would...[23]

Bayley seems to be making reference largely to Masefield's diction around the time of *The Everlasting Mercy*. A counter-argument has been made that Masefield's colloquial reality (or perceived reality) enlarged the range of expression for the Great War poets. On a more general level it is perhaps worth recording that in 1902 Masefield's first publisher, Grant Richards, was anxious about use of the word 'bloody'. Similar concerns – admittedly over a broader spectrum – were later voiced by Richards to Joyce over *Dubliners*. Robert Graves claimed that Masefield's innovation in *The Everlasting Mercy* emboldened Bernard Shaw to make the word the dramatic climax of *Pygmalion*.[24]

To counter critical attacks, we should remember that Masefield saw himself as a writer of tales, concerned with narrative. This is now deeply unfashionable. In an appreciation of Masefield, G. Wilson Knight noted 'our twentieth-century literature shows a dearth of narrative poetry'.[25] Masefield's subjects included the legends of Arthur and Troy. He was not a reactionary, but then neither were his readers. The modern critic should, I think, reflect on Masefield's popularity. The first book form of Eliot's *The Waste Land* was printed in an (American) edition of 1000 copies. In the same year the first edition of Masefield's *Collected Poems* was ten times that number. Admittedly, Eliot had previously published his work in a periodical, but the first English edition of *The Waste Land* was a mere 460 copies. Commercial popularity is not, of course, a factor in modern criticism. Yet the modern critic who decides that his views are more valuable than those of a contemporary audience is, surely, rather reckless, regardless of his critical school. Masefield's mentor was W.B. Yeats, his hero was Chaucer. He did not, necessarily, listen to critics:

> To hear these critics, one would think that the diviner qualities of art were within the reach of all, for the taking. Let them try it. That may teach them a little humility; but they know better than to try it. They know it is a good deal easier to praise or blame than to understand.[26]

Masefield's style is unfashionable. He is not a modernist or an intellectual poet. His verse is expansive in form and scope, his language, poetic form and allusions are simple and his readers are welcomed into accessible works. His focus occasionally becomes indulgent; he enjoys providing lists, his rhymes are often trite or strained and his rhythm faulty. His complete works are, moreover, vast and highly variable in quality. He is not reactionary to the past and his literary heritage. Here is a writer, however, who is engaging and eloquent. Reading Masefield is a highly rewarding, entertaining experience. He can be witty, emotionally charged and shocking. He can also spin a good yarn.

* * * *

John Masefield is no longer a contemporary poet. In the twenty-first century we might start to assess the difference between Masefield's contemporary reputation and that in which he is held today. Re-evaluation is a precious opportunity. Betjeman identified 'Sea-Fever' and 'Cargoes' as two poems that are exceptionally well-known and have entered the national consciousness. Yet after publishing 'Sea-Fever' in 1902 and 'Cargoes' in 1903 Masefield enjoyed a successful career over another half-century. If today we read Masefield because of two early poems we are surely missing something that Masefield's contemporaries saw. Should we care?

It would have been impossible for Masefield to have enjoyed a long and successful career resting on laurels earned solely from two early poems. Today we must ask why Masefield was a popular, financially successful and acclaimed writer. To facilitate this we must rescue some of his work and resist the reduction of his canon to six stanzas. If modern readers find little of interest in the works of Masefield we should, at least, reflect on the views of the author's contemporary public. Between 1923 and 1930 *Collected Poems* sold more than 100,000 copies.[27] We should care about this if we do not want a distorted view of literature in which academic disinterest deprives readers of enjoyment.

Bibliographical examination of Masefield and his work reveals that the author made a series of flawed business decisions. On numerous occasions he rejected the advances made by film companies. He resisted the interest of the popular paperback revolution and continued to drive hard bargains. He suppressed early work that had been popular and strove to control the canon of his work. Broadcasting was rarely welcomed. Increasingly, Masefield became a recluse. The public for which he had written was shunned. Several have suggested that the most fitting epitaph for Masefield was that which he wrote for the *Wanderer*:

> Mocked and deserted by the common man,
> Made half-divine to me through having failed.[28]

Writing in 1952 about second-hand book-stalls, Masefield made a statement, however, that seems particularly appropriate. The Poet Laureate wrote that 'the out-of-fashion is always cheap, and usually much better than the fashion has the wit to think.'[29]

Dr Philip W. Errington
Department of Printed Books and Manuscripts, Sotheby's

Notes

1. Daniel J. Murphy (ed.), *Lady Gregory's Journals*, Vol. I (Gerrards Cross: Colin Smythe, 1978), p. 385.
2. The only full-length biography is Constance Babington Smith, *John Masefield – A Life* (Oxford: University Press, 1978).
3. As described by Masefield within *Grace Before Ploughing* (London: Heinemann, 1966), p. 1.
4. Babington Smith, *John Masefield – A Life*, p. 32 (quoting Masefield's autobiographical sketch for Elizabeth Robins).
5. 'Nicias Moriturus' appeared in *The Outlook* on 3 June 1899. It was later included in *Salt-Water Ballads*.
6. John Masefield, letter to Harry Ross, 1 December 1902 (private collection).
7. John Masefield, *So Long to Learn* (London: Heinemann, 1952), p. 185.
8. Lord Alfred Douglas's comment is noted by Muriel Spark (see Muriel Spark, *John Masefield* (London: Peter Nevill, 1953), p. 5). Barrie's words were delivered while awarding a Royal Society of Literature prize in 1912.
9. At the Oxford Summer Diversions in 1939 Chaucer's 'The Reeve's Tale' was spoken by Tolkien 'in the costume and with the pronunciation of the time of Edward III' (see prospectus reproduced within John Gregory, *Brangwen* (Lewes: The Book Guild, 1988), p. 11).
10. *The Country Scene* (London: Collins, 1937), *A Tribute to Ballet* (London: Collins, 1938) and *A Generation Risen* (London: Collins, 1942).
11. Enid Knowles, 'Poetic Licence', *The Times*, 24 September 1982.
12. Robert Graves, 'John Masefield', *Westminster Abbey Occasional Paper No. 18* (London: Westminster Abbey, 1967), pp. 17–20.
13. See John Masefield, letter to Jack B. Yeats, 4 August 1911 (National Gallery of Ireland Yeats Archive. L.Mas.11).
14. See Fraser Drew, 'The Irish Allegiances of an English Laureate: John Masefield and Ireland', *Éire-Ireland* (Minnesota: Irish American Cultural Institute, Winter 1968), pp. 24–34 and Philip W. Errington, 'McGowan's Code: Deciphering John Masefield and Jack B. Yeats', *Yeats Annual 13* (London: Macmillan, 1998), pp. 308–16.
15. The text of 'Sea Fever' (incorrectly lacking the hyphen) appears in *Ballads and Poems* of 1910 as follows:

I must go down to the seas again, to the lonely sea and the sky,
And all I ask is a tall ship and a star to steer her by;
And the wheel's kick and the wind's song and the white sail's shaking,
And a grey mist on the sea's face, and a grey dawn breaking.

I must go down to the seas again, for the call of the running tide
Is a wild call and a clear call that may not be denied;
And all I ask is a windy day with the white clouds flying,
And the flung spray and the blown spume, and the sea-gulls crying.

I must go down to the seas again, to the vagrant gypsy life,
To the gull's way and the whale's way where the wind's like a whetted
knife;
And all I ask is a merry yarn from a laughing fellow-rover,
And quiet sleep and a sweet dream when the long trick's over.

This is the first published appearance of the text with the additional 'go'. The word is also present in the 1922 *Selected Poems*, but lacking in the 1923 *Collected Poems*. The revised collected edition of *Poems* in 1946 sees the re-appearance of the additional word.

When asked, in 1927, about the first line of the poem Masefield stated '…I notice that in the early edition, 1902, I print the line "I must down". That was as I wrote the line in the first instance. Somehow the word "go" seems to have crept in. When I am reciting the poem I usually insert the word "go". When the poem is spoken I feel the need of the word but in print "go" is unnecessary and looks ill' (see Linda Hart, 'A First Line Mystery', *The Journal of The John Masefield Society*, Vol. II (Ledbury: The John Masefield Society, 1993), pp. 11–14).

The manuscript drafts of the poem, as held in the Berg Collection of New York Public Library reveal 'I must down to the roads again…', 'I must down to the seas again…', 'I must go down to the roads again' and 'I must out on the roads again'. Two audio recordings survive of the author reading the poem. These date from 1941 and 1960 and both include the word 'go'.

16. Evidence presented within Philip W. Errington, *John Masefield – The 'Great Auk' of English Literature – A Bibliography* (London: The British Library, 2004).

17. Ibid.

18. Larkin, when awarded the Hamburg University Hanseatic Shakespeare prize described Masefield as 'a writer whose strength and simplicity I have long admired' (Philip Larkin, *Required Writing – Miscellaneous Pieces 1955-1982* (London: Faber and Faber, 1983), p. 87).

19. Shaw praised 'The Campden Wonder' (Bodleian, MS.Eng.Lett.c.255, f. 142) and, apart for the ending, Greene thought *Sard Harker* 'the greatest adventure story in the language' (Norman Sherry, *The Life of Graham Greene* (London: Cape, 1989), p. 312).

20. See illustrations in Peter Vansittart, *In the Fifties* (London: Murray, 1995),

between pp. 122–4.

21. John Betjeman, 'Preface' to John Masefield, *Selected Poems* (London: Heinemann, 1978), p. vii.
22. *The Times Literary Supplement*, 25 January 1985, p. 79.
23. *The Times Literary Supplement*, 26 April 1985, p. 469.
24. See note 12.
25. G. Wilson Knight, 'John Masefield: An Appreciation' within Geoffrey Handley-Taylor, *John Masefield...* (London: Cranbrook Tower Press, 1960), pp. 9–11.
26. Corliss and Lansing Lamont (eds.), *Letters of John Masefield to Florence Lamont* (New York: Columbia University Press, 1979), p. 82.
27. Masefield's *Collected Poems* (first published in 1923) sold 100,000 copies in the first seven years of publication, as noted by William Buchan in his 'Introduction' to *Letters to Reyna* (London: Buchan and Enright, 1983), p. 26.
28. John Masefield, 'The Wanderer', *Philip the King* (London: Heinemann, 1914), p. 67.
29. John Masefield, *So Long to Learn* (London: Heinemann, 1952), p. 93.

1899–1911

from Salt-Water Ballads

A Consecration

Not of the princes and prelates with periwigged charioteers
Riding triumphantly laurelled to lap the fat of the years, –
Rather the scorned – the rejected – the men hemmed in with the spears;

The men of the tattered battalion which fights till it dies,
Dazed with the dust of the battle, the din and the cries,
The men with the broken heads and the blood running into their eyes.

Not the be-medalled Commander, beloved of the throne,
Riding cock-horse to parade when the bugles are blown,
But the lads who carried the koppie and cannot be known.

Not the ruler for me, but the ranker, the tramp of the road,
The slave with the sack on his shoulders pricked on with the goad,
The man with too weighty a burden, too weary a load.

The sailor, the stoker of steamers, the man with the clout,
The chantyman bent at the halliards putting a tune to the shout,
The drowsy man at the wheel and the tired look-out.

Others may sing of the wine and the wealth and the mirth,
The portly presence of potentates goodly in girth; –
Mine be the dirt and the dross, the dust and scum of the earth!

THEIRS be the music, the colour, the glory, the gold;
Mine be a handful of ashes, a mouthful of mould.
Of the maimed, of the halt and the blind in the rain and the cold –

Of these shall my songs be fashioned, my tales be told.

AMEN.

I

Burial Party

'He's deader 'n nails,' the fo'c's'le said, ''n' gone to his long sleep';
''N' about his corp,' said Tom to Dan, 'd'ye think his corp'll keep
Till the day's done, 'n' the work's through, 'n' the ebb's upon the neap?'

'He's deader 'n nails,' said Dan to Tom, ''n' I wish his sperrit j'y;
He spat straight 'n' he steered true, but listen to me, say I,
Take 'n' cover 'n' bury him now, 'n' I'll take 'n' tell you why.

'It's a rummy rig of a guffy's yarn, 'n' the juice of a rummy note,
But if you buries a corp at night, it takes 'n' keeps afloat,
For its bloody soul's afraid o' the dark 'n' sticks within the throat.

''N' all the night till the grey o' the dawn the dead 'un has to swim
With a blue 'n' beastly Will o' the Wisp a-burnin' over him,
With a herring, maybe, a-scoffin' a toe or a shark a-chewin' a limb.

''N' all the night the shiverin' corp it has to swim the sea,
With its shudderin' soul inside the throat (where a soul's no right to be),
Till the sky's grey 'n' the dawn's clear, 'n' then the sperrit's free.

'Now Joe was a man was right as rain. I'm sort of sore for Joe,
'N' if we bury him durin' the day, his soul can take 'n' go;
So we'll dump his corp when the bell strikes 'n' we can get below.

'I'd fairly hate for him to swim in a blue 'n' beastly light,
With his shudderin' soul inside of him a-feelin' the fishes bite,
So over he goes at noon, say I, 'n' he shall sleep tonight.'

Bill

He lay dead on the cluttered deck and stared at the cold skies,
With never a friend to mourn for him nor a hand to close his eyes:
'Bill, he's dead,' was all they said; 'he's dead, 'n' there he lies.'

The mate came forrard at seven bells and spat across the rail:
'Just lash him up wi' some holystone in a clout o' rotten sail,
'N', rot ye, get a gait on ye, ye're slower'n a bloody snail!'

When the rising moon was a copper disc and the sea was a strip of steel,
We dumped him down to the swaying weeds ten fathom beneath the keel.
'It's rough about Bill,' the fo'c's'le said, 'we'll have to stand his wheel.'

Fever Ship

There'll be no weepin' gells ashore when *our* ship sails,
Nor no crews cheerin' us, standin' at the rails,
'N' no Blue Peter a-foul the royal stay,
For we've the Yellow Fever – Harry died to-day. –
    It's cruel when a fo'c's'le gets the fever!

'N' Dick has got the fever-shakes, 'n' look what I was told
(I went to get a sack for him to keep him from the cold):
'Sir, can I have a sack?' I says, 'for Dick 'e's fit to die.'
'Oh, sack be shot!' the skipper says, 'jest let the rotter lie!' –
    It's cruel when a fo'c's'le gets the fever!

It's a cruel port is Santos, and a hungry land,
With rows o' graves already dug in yonder strip of sand,
'N' Dick is hollerin' up the hatch, 'e says 'e's goin' blue,
His pore teeth are chattering, 'n' what's a man to do? –
    It's cruel when a fo'c's'le gets the fever!

Hell's Pavement

'When I'm discharged in Liverpool 'n' draws my bit o' pay,
I won't come to sea no more.
I'll court a pretty little lass 'n' have a weddin' day,
'N' settle somewhere down ashore.
I'll never fare to sea again a-temptin' Davy Jones,
'A-hearkening to the cruel sharks a-hungerin' for my bones;
I'll run a blushin' dairy-farm or go a-crackin' stones,
Or buy 'n' keep a little liquor-store,' –
                So he said.

They towed her in to Liverpool, we made the hooker fast,
And the copper-bound officials paid the crew,
And Billy drew his money, but the money didn't last,
For he painted the alongshore blue, –
It was rum for Poll, and rum for Nan, and gin for Jolly Jack.
He shipped a week later in the clothes upon his back,
He had to pinch a little straw, he had to beg a sack
To sleep on, when his watch was through, –
                So he did.

Sea-Change

'Oh Pythagoras – I sailed with thee last voyage.'
Herman Melville

'Goneys an' gullies an' all o' the birds o' the sea,
They ain't no birds, not really,' said Billy the Dane.
'Not mollies, nor gullies, nor goneys at all,' said he,
'But simply the sperrits of mariners livin' again.

'Them birds goin' fishin' is nothin' but souls o' the drowned,
Souls o' the drowned an' the kicked as are never no more;
An' that there haughty old albatross cruisin' around,
Belike he's Admiral Nelson or Admiral Noah.

4

'An' merry's the life they are living. They settle and dip,
They fishes, they never stands watches, they waggle their wings;
When a ship comes by, they fly to look at the ship
To see how the nowaday mariners manages things.

When freezing aloft in a snorter, I tell you I wish –
(Though maybe it ain't like a Christian) – I wish I could be
A haughty old copper-bound albatross dipping for fish
And coming the proud over all o' the birds o' the sea.

Harbour-Bar

'It was very sad about old Hal. He'd been ailing for two weeks, and died as we were towing up the river.'

An Unofficial Log

All in the feathered palm-tree tops the bright green parrots screech,
The white line of the running surf goes booming down the beach,
But I shall never see them, though the land lies close aboard,
I've shaped the last long silent tack as takes one to the Lord.

Give me the Scripters, Jakey, 'n' my pipe atween my lips,
I'm bound for somewhere south and far beyond the track of ships;
I've run my rags of colours up and clinched them to the stay,
And God the pilot's come aboard to bring me up the bay.

You'll mainsail-haul my bits o' things when Christ has took my soul,
'N' you'll lay me quiet somewhere at the landward end the Mole,
Where I shall hear the steamers' sterns a-squattering from the heave,
And the topsail blocks a-piping when a rope-yarn fouls the sheave.

Give me a sup of lime-juice; Lord, I'm drifting in to port,
The landfall lies to windward and the wind comes light and short,
And I'm for signing off and out to take my watch below,
And – prop a fellow, Jakey – Lord, it's time for me to go!

5

Nicias Moriturus

An' Bill can have my sea-boots, Nigger Jim can have my knife,
You can divvy up the dungarees an' bed,
An' the ship can have my blessing, an' the Lord can have my life,
An' sails an' fish my body when I'm dead.

An' dreaming down below there in the tangled greens an' blues,
Where the sunlight shudders golden round about,
I shall hear the ships complainin' an' the cursin' of the crews,
An' be sorry when the watch is tumbled out.

I shall hear them hilly-hollying the weather crojick brace,
And the sucking of the wash about the hull;
When they chanty up the topsail I'll be hauling in my place,
For my soul will follow seawards like a gull.

I shall hear the blocks a-grunting in the bumpkins over-side,
An' the slatting of the storm-sails on the stay,
An' the rippling of the catspaw at the making of the tide,
An' the swirl and splash of porpoises at play.

An' Bill can have my sea-boots, Nigger Jim can have my knife,
You can divvy up the whack I haven't scofft,
An' the ship can have my blessing and the Lord can have my life,
For it's time I quit the deck and went aloft.

A Night at Dago Tom's

Oh yesterday, I t'ink it was, while cruisin' down the street,
I met with Bill. – 'Hullo,' he says, 'let's give the girls a treat.'
We'd red bandanas round our necks 'n' our shrouds new rattled down,
So we filled a couple of Santy Cruz and cleared for Sailor Town.

We scooted south with a press of sail till we fetched to a caboose,
The 'Sailor's Rest,' by Dago Tom, alongside 'Paddy's Goose.'
Red curtains to the windies, ay, 'n' white sand to the floor,
And an old blind fiddler liltin' the tune of 'Lowlands no more.'

He played the 'Shaking of the Sheets' 'n' the couples did advance,
Bowing, stamping, curtsying, in the shuffling of the dance;
The old floor rocked and quivered, so it struck beholders dumb,
'N' arterwards there was sweet songs 'n' good Jamaikey rum.

'N' there was many a merry yarn of many a merry spree
Aboard the ships with royals set a-sailing on the sea,
Yarns of the hooker 'Spindrift,' her as had the clipper-bow, –
'There ain't no ships,' says Bill to me, 'like that there hooker now.'

When the old blind fiddler played the tune of 'Pipe the Watch Below,'
The skew-eyed landlord dowsed the glim and bade us 'stamp 'n' go,'
'N' we linked it home, did Bill 'n' I, adown the scattered streets,
Until we fetched to Land o' Nod atween the linen sheets.

'Port o' Many Ships'

'It's a sunny pleasant anchorage, is Kingdom Come,
Where crews is always layin' aft for double-tots o' rum,
'N' there's dancin' 'n' fiddlin' of ev'ry kind o' sort,
It's a fine place for sailor-men is that there port.
        'N' I wish –
        I wish as I was there.

'The winds is never nothin' more than jest light airs,
'N' no-one gets belayin'-pinned, 'n' no-one never swears,
Yer free to loaf an' laze around, yer pipe atween yer lips,
Lollin' on the fo'c's'le, sonny, lookin' at the ships.
        'N' I wish –
        I wish as I was there.

'For ridin' in the anchorage the ships of all the world
Have got one anchor down 'n' all sails furled.
All the sunken hookers 'n' the crews as took 'n' died
They lays there merry, sonny, swingin' to the tide.
      'N' I wish –
      I wish as I was there.

'Drowned old wooden hookers green wi' drippin' wrack,
Ships as never fetched to port, as never came back,
Swingin' to the blushin' tide, dippin' to the swell,
'N' the crews all singin', sonny, beatin' on the bell.
      'N' I wish –
      I wish as I was there.'

Mother Carey

(As Told Me by the Bo'sun)

Mother Carey? She's the mother o' the witches
'N' all *them* sort o' rips;
She's a fine gell to look at, but the hitch is,
She's a sight too fond of ships.
She lives upon a iceberg to the norred,
An' her man he's Davy Jones,
'N' she combs the weeds upon her forred
With pore drowned sailors' bones.

She's the mother o' the wrecks, 'n' the mother
Of all big winds as blows;
She's up to some deviltry or other
When it storms, or sleets, or snows.
The noise of the wind's her screamin',
'I'm arter a plump, young, fine,
Brass-buttoned, beefy-ribbed young seam'n
So as me 'n' my mate kin dine.'

She's a hungry old rip 'n' a cruel
For sailor-men like we,
She's give a many mariners the gruel
'N' a long sleep under sea.
She's the blood o' many a crew upon her
'N' the bones of many a wreck,
'N' she's barnacles a-growin' on her
'N' shark's teeth round her neck.

I ain't never had no schoolin'
Nor read no books like you,
But I knows 't ain't healthy to be foolin'
With that there gristly two.
You're young, you thinks, 'n' you're lairy,
But if you're to make old bones,
Steer clear, I says, o' Mother Carey
'N' that there Davy Jones.

Trade Winds

In the harbour, in the island, in the Spanish Seas,
Are the tiny white houses and the orange-trees,
And day-long, night-long, the cool and pleasant breeze
Of the steady Trade Winds blowing.

There is the red wine, the nutty Spanish ale,
The shuffle of the dancers, the old salt's tale,
The squeaking fiddle, and the soughing in the sail
Of the steady Trade Winds blowing.

And o' nights there's fire-flies and the yellow moon,
And in the ghostly palm-trees the sleepy tune
Of the quiet voice calling me, the long low croon
Of the steady Trade Winds blowing.

Sea-Fever

I must down to the seas again, to the lonely sea and the sky,
And all I ask is a tall ship and a star to steer her by,
And the wheel's kick and the wind's song and the white sail's shaking,
And a grey mist on the sea's face and a grey dawn breaking.

I must down to the seas again, for the call of the running tide
Is a wild call and a clear call that may not be denied;
And all I ask is a windy day with the white clouds flying,
And the flung spray and the blown spume, and the sea-gulls crying.

I must down to the seas again to the vagrant gypsy life,
To the gull's way and the whale's way where the wind's like a whetted knife;
And all I ask is a merry yarn from a laughing fellow-rover,
And quiet sleep and a sweet dream when the long trick's over.

A Wanderer's Song

For W.B. Yeats

A wind's in the heart o' me, a fire's in my heels,
I am tired of brick and stone and rumbling wagon-wheels;
I hunger for the sea's edge, the limits of the land,
Where the wild old Atlantic is shouting on the sand.

Oh I'll be going, leaving the noises of the street,
To where a lifting foresail-foot is yanking at the sheet;
To a windy, tossing anchorage where yawls and ketches ride,
Oh I'll be going, going, until I meet the tide.

And first I'll hear the sea-wind, the mewing of the gulls,
The clucking, sucking of the sea about the rusty hulls,
The songs at the capstan in the hooker warping out,
And then the heart of me'll know I'm there or thereabout.

Oh I am tired of brick and stone, the heart o' me is sick,
For windy green, unquiet sea, the realm o' Moby Dick;
And I'll be going, going, from the roaring of the wheels,
For a wind's in the heart o' me, a fire's in my heels.

Cardigan Bay

For Laurence Binyon

Clean, green, windy billows notching out the sky,
Grey clouds tattered into rags, sea-winds blowing high,
And the ships under topsails, beating, thrashing by,
And the mewing of the herring gulls.

Dancing, flashing green seas shaking white locks,
Boiling in blind eddies over hidden rocks,
And the wind in the rigging, the creaking o' the blocks,
And the straining of the timber hulls.

Delicate, cool sea-weeds, green and amber-brown,
In beds where shaken sunlight slowly filters down
On many a drowned seventy-four, many a sunken town,
And the whitening of the dead men's skulls.

The Tarry Buccaneer

For Jack B. Yeats

Air – 'The Fine Old English Gentleman'

I'm going to be a pirate with a bright brass pivot-gun,
And an island in the Spanish Main beyond the setting sun,
And a silver flagon full of red wine to drink when work is done,
Like a fine old salt-sea scavenger, like a tarry Buccaneer.

With a sandy creek to careen in, and a pig-tailed Spanish mate,
And under my main-hatches a sparkling merry freight
Of doubloons and double moidores and pieces of eight,
Like a fine old salt-sea scavenger, like a tarry Buccaneer.

With a taste for Spanish wine-shops and for spending my doubloons,
And a crew of swart mulattoes and black-eyed octoroons,
And a thoughtful way with mutineers of making them maroons,
Like a fine old salt-sea scavenger, like a tarry Buccaneer.

With a sash of crimson velvet and a diamond-hilted sword,
And a silver whistle about my neck secured to a golden cord,
And a habit of taking captives and walking them along a board,
Like a fine old salt-sea scavenger, like a tarry Buccaneer.

With a spy-glass tucked beneath my arm and a cocked hat cocked askew,
And a long low rakish schooner a-cutting of the waves in two,
And a flag of skull and cross-bones the wickedest that ever flew,
Like a fine old salt-sea scavenger, like a tarry Buccaneer.

A Ballad of John Silver

We were schooner-rigged and rakish, with a long and lissome hull,
And we flew the pretty colours of the cross-bones and the skull;
We'd a big black Jolly Roger flapping grimly at the fore,
And we sailed the Spanish Water in the happy days of yore.

We'd a long brass gun amidships, like a well-conducted ship,
We had each a brace of pistols and a cutlass at the hip;
It's a point which tells against us, and a fact to be deplored,
But we chased the goodly merchant-men and laid their ships aboard.

Then the dead men fouled the scuppers and the wounded filled the chains,
And the paint-work all was spatter-dashed with other people's brains,
She was boarded, she was looted, she was scuttled till she sank,
And the pale survivors left us by the medium of the plank.

O! then it was (while standing by the taffrail on the poop)
We could hear the drowning folk lament the absent chicken-coop;
Then, having washed the blood away, we'd little else to do
Than to dance a quiet hornpipe as the old salts taught us to.

O! the fiddle on the fo'c's'le, and the slapping naked soles,
And the genial 'Down the middle, Jake, and curtsy when she rolls!'
With the silver seas around us and the pale moon overhead,
And the look-out not a-looking and his pipe-bowl glowing red.

Ah! the pig-tailed, quidding pirates and the pretty pranks we played,
All have since been put a stop-to by the naughty Board of Trade;
The schooners and the merry crews are laid away to rest,
A little south the sunset in the Islands of the Blest.

The West Wind

It's a warm wind, the west wind, full of birds' cries;
I never hear the west wind but tears are in my eyes.
For it comes from the west lands, the old brown hills,
And April's in the west wind, and daffodils.

It's a fine land, the west land, for hearts as tired as mine,
Apple orchards blossom there, and the air's like wine.
There is cool green grass there, where men may lie at rest,
And the thrushes are in song there, fluting from the nest.

'Will ye not come home, brother? ye have been long away,
It's April, and blossom time, and white is the may;
And bright is the sun, brother, and warm is the rain, –
Will ye not come home, brother, home to us again?

'The young corn is green, brother, where the rabbits run,
It's blue sky, and white clouds, and warm rain and sun.
It's song to a man's soul, brother, fire to a man's brain,
To hear the wild bees and see the merry spring again.

'Larks are singing in the west, brother, above the green wheat,
So will ye not come home, brother, and rest your tired feet?
I've a balm for bruised hearts, brother, sleep for aching eyes,'
Says the warm wind, the west wind, full of birds' cries.

It's the white road westwards is the road I must tread
To the green grass, the cool grass, and rest for heart and head,
To the violets and the warm hearts and the thrushes' song,
In the fine land, the west land, the land where I belong.

Sorrow o' Mydath

Weary the cry of the wind is, weary the sea,
Weary the heart and the mind and the body o' me.
Would I were out of it, done with it, would I could be
A white gull crying along the desolate sands!

Outcast, derelict soul in a body accurst,
Standing drenched with the spindrift, standing athirst,
For the cool green waves of death to arise and burst
In a tide of quiet for me on the desolate sands.

Would that the waves and the long white hair o' the spray
Would gather in splendid terror and blot me away
To the sunless place o' the wrecks where the waters sway
Gently, dreamily, quietly over desolate sands!

Vagabond

Dunno a heap about the what an' why,
Can't say's I ever knowed.
Heaven to me's a fair blue stretch of sky,
Earth's jest a dusty road.

Dunno the names o' things, nor what they are,
Can't say's I ever will.
Dunno about God – He's jest the noddin' star
Atop the windy hill.

Dunno about Life – it's jest a tramp alone
From wakin'-time to doss.
Dunno about Death – it's jest a quiet stone
All over-grey wi' moss.

An' why I live, an' why the old world spins,
Are things I never knowed;
My mark's the gypsy fires, the lonely inns,
An' jest the dusty road.

Spunyarn

Spunyarn, spunyarn, with one to turn the crank,
And one to slather the spunyarn, and one to knot the hank;
It's an easy job for a summer watch, and a pleasant job enough,
To twist the tarry lengths of yarn to shapely sailor stuff.

Life is nothing but spunyarn on a winch in need of oil,
Little enough is twined and spun but fever-fret and moil.
I have travelled on land and sea, and all that I have found
Are these poor songs to brace the arms that help the winches round.

Personal

Tramping at night in the cold and wet, I passed the lighted inn,
And an old tune, a sweet tune, was being played within.
It was full of the laugh of the leaves and the song the wind sings;
It brought the tears and the choked throat, and a catch to the heart-strings.

And it brought a bitter thought of the days that now were dead to me,
The merry days in the old home before I went to sea –
Days that were dead to me indeed. I bowed my head to the rain,
And I passed by the lighted inn to the lonely roads again.

On Eastnor Knoll

Silent are the woods, and the dim green boughs are
Hushed in the twilight: yonder, in the path through
The apple orchard, is a tired plough-boy
Calling the kine home.

A bright white star blinks, the pale moon rounds, but
Still the red, lurid wreckage of the sunset
Smoulders in smoky fire, and burns on
The misty hill-tops.

Ghostly it grows, and darker, the burning
Fades into smoke, and now the gusty oaks are
A silent army of phantoms thronging
A land of shadows.

'All Ye That Pass By'

On the long dusty ribbon of the long city street,
The pageant of life is passing me on multitudinous feet,
With a word here of the hills, and a song there of the sea,
And – the great movement changes – the pageant passes me.

Faces – passionate faces – of men I may not know,
They haunt me, burn me to the heart, as I turn aside to go:
The king's face and the cur's face, and the face of the stuffed swine,
They are passing, they are passing, their eyes look into mine.

I never can tire of the music of the noise of many feet,
The thrill of the blood pulsing, the tick of the heart's beat,
Of the men many as sands, of the squadrons ranked and massed
Who are passing, changing always, and never have changed or passed.

In Memory of A.P.R.

Once in the windy wintry weather,
The road dust blowing in our eyes,
We starved and tramped or slept together
Beneath the haystacks and the skies;

Until the tiring tramp was over,
And then the wind for him was blown,
He left his friend – his fellow-rover –
To tramp the dusty roads alone.

The winds wail and the woods are yellow,
The hills are blotted in the rain,
'And would he were with me,' sighs his fellow,
'With me upon the roads again!'

from Ballads

The Ballad of Sir Bors

Would I could win some quiet and rest, and a little ease,
In the cool grey hush of the dusk, in the dim green place of the trees,
Where the birds are singing, singing, singing, crying aloud
The song of the red, red rose that blossoms beyond the seas.

Would I could see it, the rose, when the light begins to fail,
And a lone white star in the West is glimmering on the mail;
The red, red passionate rose of the sacred blood of the Christ,
In the shining chalice of God, the cup of the Holy Grail.

The dusk comes gathering grey, and the darkness dims the West,
The oxen low to the byre, and all bells ring to rest;
But I ride over the moors, for the dusk still bides and waits,
That brims my soul with the glow of the rose that ends the Quest.

My horse is spavined and ribbed, and his bones come through his hide,
My sword is rotten with rust, but I shake the reins and ride,
For the bright white birds of God that nest in the rose have called,
And never a township now is a town where I can bide.

It will happen at last, at dusk, as my horse limps down the fell,
A star will glow like a note God strikes on a silver bell,
And the bright white birds of God will carry my soul to Christ,
And the sight of the Rose, the Rose, will pay for the years of hell.

Spanish Waters

Air – 'Sir Harry Lingen's Riding'

Spanish waters, Spanish waters, you are ringing in my ears,
Like a sweet quaint piece of music from the grey forgotten years;
Telling tales, and weaving runes, and bringing weary thoughts to me
Of the sandy beach at Muertos, where I would that I could be.

Oh the sunny beach at Muertos, and the windy spit of sand,
Off of which we came to anchor while the shipmates went a-land;
Where the blue laguna emptied over snags of rotting trees,
And the golden sunlight quivered on the brilliant colibris.

We came to port at Muertos when the dipping sun was red,
And we moored her half-a-mile to sea, to west of Nigger Head;
And before the mist was on the Key, before the day was done,
We put ashore to Muertos with the gold that we had won.

We bore it through the marshes in a half-score battered chests,
Sinking, staggering in the quagmire till the lush weed touched the breasts,
While the slithering feet were squelching in the pulp of fallen fruits,
And the cold and clammy leeches bit and sucked us through the boots.

The moon came white and ghostly as we laid the treasure down,
All the spoil of scuttled carracks, all the loot of Lima Town.
Copper charms and silver trinkets from the chests of perished crews,
Gold doubloons and double moydores, louis d'ors and portagues.

Clumsy yellow-metal earrings from the Indians of Brazil,
Emerald ouches out of Rio, silver bars from Guyaquil,
Silver cups and polished flagons, censers wrought in flowered bronze,
And the chased enamelled sword hilts of the courtly Spanish Dons.

We smoothed the place with mattocks, and we took and blazed the tree,
Which marks you where the gold is hid that none will ever see,
And we laid aboard the brig again, and south away we steers,
Through the loud white surf of Muertos which is beating in my ears.

I'm the last alive that knows it. All the rest were took and swung
In chains at Execution Dock, where thieves and such are hung,
And I go singing, fiddling, old and starved and castaway,
And I know where all the gold is that we won with L'Ollonais.

Well, I've had a merry life of it. I'm old and nearly blind,
But the sun-dried swinging shipmates' chains are clanking in my mind;
And I see in dreams, awhiles, the beach, the sun's disc dipping red,
And the tall brig, under topsails, swaying in past Nigger Head.

I'd be glad to step ashore there. Glad to take a pick and go
To the lone blazed coco-palm tree in the place no others know,
And lift the gold and silver that has mouldered there for years
By the loud white surf of Muertos which is beating in my ears.

Cargoes

Quinquireme of Nineveh from distant Ophir,
Rowing home to haven in sunny Palestine,
With a cargo of ivory,
And apes and peacocks,
Sandalwood, cedarwood, and sweet white wine.

Stately Spanish galleon coming from the Isthmus,
Dipping through the Tropics by the palm-green shores,
With a cargo of diamonds,
Emeralds, amethysts,
Topazes, and cinnamon, and gold moidores.

Dirty British coaster with a salt-caked smoke stack,
Butting through the Channel in the mad March days,
With a cargo of Tyne coal,
Road-rails, pig-lead,
Firewood, ironware, and cheap tin trays.

Captain Stratton's Fancy

Air – 'Masefield's Own'

Oh some are fond of red wine, and some are fond of white,
And some are all for dancing by the pale moonlight,
But rum alone's the tipple, and the heart's delight
Of the old bold mate of Henry Morgan.

Oh some are fond of Spanish wine, and some are fond of French,
And some'll swallow tay and stuff fit only for a wench,
But I'm for right Jamaica till I roll beneath the bench,
Says the old bold mate of Henry Morgan.

Oh some are for the lily, and some are for the rose,
But I am for the sugar-cane that in Jamaica grows.
For it's that that makes the bonny drink to warm my copper nose,
Says the old bold mate of Henry Morgan.

Oh some are fond of fiddles, and a song well sung.
And some are all for music for to lilt upon the tongue;
But mouths were made for tankards, and for sucking at the bung,
Says the old bold mate of Henry Morgan.

Oh some are fond of dancing, and some are fond of dice,
And some are all for red lips, and pretty lasses' eyes;
But a right Jamaica puncheon is a finer prize
To the old bold mate of Henry Morgan.

Oh some that's good and godly ones they hold that it's a sin,
To troll the jolly bowl around, and let the dollars spin;
But I'm for toleration, and for drinking at an inn,
Says the old bold mate of Henry Morgan.

Oh some are sad and wretched folk that go in silken suits,
And there's a mort of wicked rogues that live in good reputes;
So I'm for drinking honestly, and dying in my boots,
Like an old bold mate of Henry Morgan.

St Mary's Bells

Air – 'Manzanares'

It's pleasant in Holy Mary
By San Marie lagoon,
The bells they chime and jingle
From dawn to afternoon.
They rhyme and chime and mingle,
They pulse and boom and beat,
And the laughing bells are gentle
And the mournful bells are sweet.

Oh, who are the men that ring them,
The bells of San Marie,
Oh, who but sonsie seamen
Come in from over sea,
And merrily in the belfries
They rock and sway and hale,
And send the bells a-jangle,
And down the lusty ale.

It's pleasant in Holy Mary
To hear the beaten bells
Come booming into music,
Which throbs, and clangs, and swells,
From sunset till the daybreak,
From dawn to afternoon.
In port of Holy Mary
On San Marie Lagoon.

London Town

Air – 'Bradlow Knoll'

Oh London Town's a fine town, and London sights are rare,
And London ale is right ale, and brisk's the London air,
And busily goes the world there, but crafty grows the mind,
And London Town of all towns I'm glad to leave behind.

Then hey for croft and hop-yard, and hill, and field, and pond,
With Bredon Hill before me and Malvern Hill beyond.
The hawthorn white i' the hedgerow, and all the spring's attire
In the comely land of Teme and Lugg, and Clent and Clee, and Wyre.

Oh London girls are brave girls, in silk and cloth o' gold,
And London shops are rare shops, where gallant things are sold,
And bonnily clinks the gold there, but drowsily blinks the eye,
And London Town of all towns I'm glad to hurry by.

Then, hey for covert and woodland, and ash and elm and oak,
Tewkesbury inns, and Malvern roofs, and Worcester chimney smoke,
The red-felled Hereford cattle a-lowing from field and byre,
And Bradlow Knoll, and Kilbury Camp, and Ledbury Church's spire.

Oh London tunes are new tunes, and London books are wise,
And London plays are rare plays, and fine to country eyes,
Wretchedly fare the most there, and happily fare the few,
And London Town of all towns I'm glad to hurry through.

So hey for the road, the west road, by mill and forge and fold,
Scent of the fern and song of the lark by brook, and field, and wold,
To the comely folk at the hearth-stone and the ale beside the fire,
In the hearty land, the home land, my land of heart's desire.

The Emigrant

Air – 'The Ships in Gara River'

Going by Daly's shanty I heard the boys within
Dancing the Spanish hornpipe to Driscoll's violin,
I heard the sea-boots shaking the rough planks of the floor,
But I was going westward, I hadn't heart for more.

All down the windy village the noise rang in my ears,
Old sea boots stamping, shuffling, bringing the bitter tears,
The old tune piped and quavered, the lilts came clear and strong,
But I was going westward, I couldn't join the song.

There were the grey stone houses, the night wind blowing keen,
The hill-sides pale with moonlight, the young corn springing green,
The hearth nooks lit and kindly, with dear friends good to see,
But I was going westward, and the ship waited me.

The Seekers

Friends and loves we have none, nor wealth, nor blessed abode,
But the hope, the burning hope, and the road, the lonely road.

Not for us are content, and quiet, and peace of mind,
For we go seeking cities that we shall never find.

There is no solace on earth for us – for such as we –
Who search for the hidden beauty that eyes may never see.

Only the road and the dawn, the sun, the wind, and the rain,
And the watch-fire under stars, and sleep, and the road again.

We seek the City of God, and the haunt where beauty dwells,
And we find the noisy mart and the sound of burial bells.

Never the golden city, where radiant people meet,
But the dolorous town where mourners are going about the street.

We travel the dusty road till the light of the day is dim,
And sunset shows us spires away on the world's rim.

We travel from dawn to dusk, till the day is past and by,
Seeking the Holy City beyond the rim of the sky.

Friends and loves we have none, nor wealth nor blest abode,
But the hope, the burning hope, and the road, the lonely road.

Hall Sands

The village of Hall Sands, between Dartmouth and Start Point, in South Devonshire, is imminently threatened by the sea. Its natural breakwater of sand and shingle was removed a few months ago by a Government contractor, and since its removal the sea has encroached upon the foreshore, and is now undermining some of the houses.

The land on which the village stands is beginning to slip and settle. The sea takes a heavy toll of earth at each high tide. The fishermen are in danger of utter ruin, and the first gale from the south-east is likely to sweep the village from its site.

The moon is bright on Devon sands,
The pale moon brings the tide,
The cold green water's greedy hands
Are clutching far and wide
Where the brown nets are dried.

Oh! snaky are the salt green waves
That wash the scattered shells;
They come from making sailors' graves
And tolling sunk ships' bells –
But now their tossing swells

Are lipping greedy at the stone
Which props the scattered town.
They cannot leave the rocks alone,
They mean to sink and drown
The wretched cabins down.

The beams are creaking, and the walls
Are cracking, while the sea
Lips landward steadily and galls
Those huts of brick and tree
Which men's homes used to be.

Lithe, wicked eddies twist and spin
Where once they dragged the boats.
The nimble shrimps are nesting in
The rye-patch – and the throats
Of sea-snails glut the oats.

It is all falling, slipping swift;
The thievish tides intend
To crumble down and set adrift,
To eat away, and rend.
And steal, and make an end.

Soon, when the wind is setting cold
And sharp from the south-east,
The great salt water running bold
Will give the fish a feast,
And the town will have ceased,

But that its wretched ruins then –
Though sunken utterly –
Will show how the brute greed of men
Helps feed the greedy sea.

Laugh and be Merry

Laugh and be merry, remember, better the world with a song,
Better the world with a blow in the teeth of a wrong.
Laugh for the time is brief, a thread the length of a span.
Laugh and be proud to belong to the old proud pageant of man.

Laugh and be merry: remember, in olden time,
God made Heaven and Earth for joy He took in a rhyme,
Made them, and filled them full with the strong red wine of His mirth,
The splendid joy of the stars: the joy of the earth.

So we must laugh and drink from the deep blue cup of the sky
Join the jubilant song of the great stars sweeping by,
Laugh, and battle, and work, and drink of the wine outpoured
In the dear green earth, the sign of the joy of the Lord.

Laugh and be merry together, like brothers akin,
Guesting awhile in the rooms of a beautiful inn,
Glad till the dancing stops, and the lilt of the music ends.
Laugh till the game is played; and be you merry, my friends.

Blind Man's Vigil

Mumblin' under the gallows, hearin' the clank o' the chain,
Hearin' the suck o' the sea as the tide goes by the stair,
I fiddles a lilt o' tune to the bones o' the men o' the Main,
Who dangle, rattle, and dance in the rusty chains on air.

Poor old mariners' bones, a mark for cobbles and hoys,
As they go about in the Reach when the dingy tide's at flood.
Bones of Billy's old shipmates, bones o' the merry boys,
Whose faults were dollars and girls, and a too quick tick o' the blood.

They wasn't the lads to rest in a patch of Christian mould,
Under a marble slab with a verse o' Scripter to 't.
They asked for liquor, an' fun, an' a friend to share the gold,
An' a dance in hemp at last wi' nothin' but air to foot.

I fiddles 'em bits o' tunes, an' ballads, an' songs, an' rhymes,
Of the sort that brought the anchor home, an' the yard to the masthead;
An' I think they likes to hear, for it makes 'em mind the times,
When the blood was hot, an' the throat was dry, an' a woman's lips
                                                        were red.

Fiddlin' under the gallows I mumbles tunes an' words
To the danglin', janglin' rags an' bones that once were lads I knew;
(An' I think they likes to hear), an' it scares away the birds,
From the men who go where the wind blows, an' went where the
                                                        wind blew.

Roadways

One road leads to London,
One road runs to Wales,
My road leads me seawards
To the white dipping sails.
One road leads to the river,
As it goes singing slow;
My road leads to shipping,
Where the bronzed sailors go.

Leads me, lures me, calls me
To salt green tossing sea;
A road without earth's road-dust
Is the right road for me.
A wet road heaving, shining,
And wild with sea-gulls' cries,
A mad salt sea-wind blowing
The salt spray in my eyes.

My road calls me, lures me
West, east, south, and north;
Most roads lead men homewards,
My road leads me forth
To add more miles to the tally
Of grey miles left behind,
In quest of that one beauty
God put me here to find.

from A Mainsail Haul

['I yarned with ancient shipmen...']

I yarned with ancient shipmen beside the galley range,
And some were fond of women, but all were fond of change;
They sang their quavering chanties, all in a fo'c's'le drone,
And I was finely suited, if I had only known.

I rested in an ale-house that had a sanded floor,
Where seamen sat a-drinking and chalking up the score;
They yarned of ships and mermaids, of topsail sheets and slings,
But I was discontented: I looked for better things.

I heard a drunken fiddler, in Billy Lee's Saloon,
I brooked an empty belly with thinking of the tune:
The beer-mugs clanked approval, the drunkards rose to dance,
And now I know the music was life and life's romance.

from Ballads (second edition)

Twilight

Twilight it is, and the far woods are dim, and the rooks cry and call.
Down in the valley the lamps, and the mist, and a star over all,
There by the rick, where they thresh, is the drone at an end,
Twilight it is, and I travel the road with my friend.

I think of the friends who are dead, who were dear long ago in the past,
Beautiful friends who are dead, though I know that death cannot last;
Friends with the beautiful eyes that the dust has defiled,
Beautiful souls who were gentle when I was a child.

from Ballads and Poems

Posted as Missing

Under all her topsails she trembled like a stag,
The wind made a ripple in her bonny red flag;
They cheered her from the shore and they cheered her from the pier,
And under all her topsails she trembled like a deer.

So she passed swaying, where the green seas run,
Her wind-steadied topsails were stately in the sun;
There was glitter on the water from her red port light,
So she passed swaying, till she was out of sight.

Long and long ago it was, a weary time it is,
The bones of her sailor-men are coral plants by this;
Coral plants, and shark-weed, and a mermaid's comb,
And if the fishers net them they never bring them home.

It's rough on sailors' women. They have to mangle hard,
And stitch at dungarees till their finger-ends are scarred,
Thinking of the sailor-men who sang among the crowd,
Hoisting of her topsails when she sailed so proud.

A Creed

I hold that when a person dies
His soul returns again to earth;
Arrayed in some new flesh-disguise
Another mother gives him birth.
With sturdier limbs and brighter brain
The old soul takes the roads again.

Such is my own belief and trust;
This hand, this hand that holds the pen,
Has many a hundred times been dust
And turned, as dust, to dust again;
These eyes of mine have blinked and shone
In Thebes, in Troy, in Babylon.

All that I rightly think or do,
Or make, or spoil, or bless, or blast,
Is curse or blessing justly due
For sloth or effort in the past.
My life's a statement of the sum
Of vice indulged, or overcome.

I know that in my lives to be
My sorry heart will ache and burn,
And worship, unavailingly,
The woman whom I used to spurn,
And shake to see another have
The love I spurned, the love she gave.

And I shall know, in angry words,
In gibes, and mocks, and many a tear,
A carrion flock of homing-birds,
The gibes and scorns I uttered here.
The brave word that I failed to speak
Will brand me dastard on the cheek.

And as I wander on the roads
I shall be helped and healed and blessed;
Dear words shall cheer and be as goads
To urge to heights before unguessed.
My road shall be the road I made;
All that I gave shall be repaid.

So shall I fight, so shall I tread,
In this long war beneath the stars;
So shall a glory wreathe my head,
So shall I faint and show the scars,
Until this case, this clogging mould,
Be smithied all to kingly gold.

When Bony Death

When bony Death has chilled her gentle blood,
And dimmed the brightness of her wistful eyes,
And changed her glorious beauty into mud
By his old skill in hateful wizardries;

When an old lichened marble strives to tell
How sweet a grace, how red a lip was hers;
When rheumy grey-beards say, 'I knew her well,'
Showing the grave to curious worshippers;

When all the roses that she sowed in me
Have dripped their crimson petals and decayed,
Leaving no greenery on any tree
That her dear hands in my heart's garden laid,

Then grant, old Time, to my green mouldering skull,
These songs may keep her memory beautiful.

Being her Friend

Being her friend, I do not care, not I,
How gods or men may wrong me, beat me down;
Her word's sufficient star to travel by,
I count her quiet praise sufficient crown.

Being her friend, I do not covet gold,
Save for a royal gift to give her pleasure;
To sit with her, and have her hand to hold,
Is wealth, I think, surpassing minted treasure.

Being her friend, I only covet art,
A white pure flame to search me as I trace
In crooked letters from a throbbing heart,
The hymn to beauty written on her face.

33

Fragments

Troy Town is covered up with weeds,
The rabbits and the pismires brood
On broken gold, and shards, and beads
Where Priam's ancient palace stood.

The floors of many a gallant house
Are matted with the roots of grass;
The glow-worm and the nimble mouse
Among her ruins flit and pass.

And there, in orts of blackened bone,
The widowed Trojan beauties lie,
And Simois babbles over stone
And waps and gurgles to the sky.

Once there were merry days in Troy,
Her chimneys smoked with cooking meals,
The passing chariots did annoy
The sunning housewives at their wheels.

And many a lovely Trojan maid
Set Trojan lads to lovely things;
The game of life was nobly played,
They played the game like Queens and Kings.

So that, when Troy had greatly passed
In one red roaring fiery coal,
The courts the Grecians overcast
Became a city in the soul.

In some green island of the sea,
Where now the shadowy coral grows
In pride and pomp and empery
The courts of old Atlantis rose.

In many a glittering house of glass
The Atlanteans wandered there;
The paleness of their faces was
Like ivory, so pale they were.

And hushed they were, no noise of words
In those bright cities ever rang;
Only their thoughts, like golden birds,
About their chambers thrilled and sang.

They knew all wisdom, for they knew
The souls of those Egyptian Kings
Who learned, in ancient Babilu,
The beauty of immortal things.

They knew all beauty – when they thought
The air chimed like a striken lyre,
The elemental birds were wrought,
The golden birds became a fire.

And straight to busy camps and marts
The singing flames were swiftly gone;
The trembling leaves of human hearts
Hid boughs for them to perch upon.

And men in desert places, men
Abandoned, broken, sick with fears,
Rose singing, swung their swords agen,
And laughed and died among the spears.

The green and greedy seas have drowned
That city's glittering walls and towers,
Her sunken minarets are crowned
With red and russet water-flowers.

In towers and rooms and golden courts
The shadowy coral lifts her sprays;
The scrawl hath gorged her broken orts,
The shark doth haunt her hidden ways.

But, at the falling of the tide,
The golden birds still sing and gleam,
The Atlanteans have not died,
Immortal things still give us dream.

The dream that fires man's heart to make,
To build, to do, to sing or say
A beauty Death can never take,
An Adam from the crumbled clay.

The Death Rooms

My soul has many an old decaying room
Hung with the ragged arras of the past,
Where startled faces flicker in the gloom,
And horrid whispers set the cheek aghast.

Those dropping rooms are haunted by a death,
A something like a worm gnawing a brain,
That bids me heed what bitter lesson saith,
The blind wind beating on the window-pane.

None dwells in those old rooms: none ever can –
I pass them through at night with hidden head;
Lock'd rotting rooms her eyes must never scan,
Floors that her blessed feet must never tread.

Haunted old rooms: rooms she must never know,
Where death-ticks knock and mouldering panels glow.

C.L.M.

In the dark womb where I began
My mother's life made me a man.
Through all the months of human birth
Her beauty fed my common earth.
I cannot see, nor breathe, nor stir,
But through the death of some of her.

Down in the darkness of the grave
She cannot see the life she gave.
For all her love, she cannot tell
Whether I use it ill or well,
Nor knock at dusty doors to find
Her beauty dusty in the mind.

If the grave's gates could be undone,
She would not know her little son,
I am so grown. If we should meet
She would pass by me in the street,
Unless my soul's face let her see
My sense of what she did for me.

What have I done to keep in mind
My debt to her and womankind?
What woman's happier life repays
Her for those months of wretched days?
For all my mouthless body leeched
Ere Birth's releasing hell was reached?

What have I done, or tried, or said
In thanks to that dear woman dead?
Men triumph over women still,
Men trample women's rights at will,
And man's lust roves the world untamed.

* * * *

O grave, keep shut lest I be shamed.

Waste

No rose but fades: no glory but must pass:
No hue but dims: no precious silk but frets.
Her beauty must go underneath the grass,
Under the long roots of the violets.

O, many glowing beauties Time has hid
In that dark, blotting box the villain sends.
He covers over with a coffin-lid
Mothers and sons, and foes and lovely friends.

Maids that were redly-lipped and comely-skinned,
Friends that deserved a sweeter bed than clay,
All are as blossoms blowing down the wind,
Things the old envious villain sweeps away.

And though the mutterer laughs and church bells toll,
Death brings another April to the soul.

Third Mate

All the sheets are clacking, all the blocks are whining,
The sails are frozen stiff and the wetted decks are shining;
The reef's in the topsails, and its coming on to blow,
And I think of the dear girl I left long ago.

Grey were her eyes, and her hair was long and bonny,
Golden was her hair, like the wild bees' honey.
And I was but a dog, and a mad one to despise,
The gold of her hair and the grey of her eyes.

There's the sea before me, and my home's behind me,
And beyond there the strange lands where nobody will mind me,
No one but the girls with the paint upon their cheeks,
Who sell away their beauty to whomsoever seeks.

There'll be drink and women there, and songs and laughter,
Peace from what is past and from all that follows after;
And a fellow will forget how a woman lies awake,
Lonely in the night watch crying for his sake.

Black it blows and bad and it howls like slaughter,
And the ship she shudders as she takes the water.
Hissing flies the spindrift like a wind-blown smoke,
And I think of a woman and a heart I broke.

Christmas, 1903

O, the sea breeze will be steady, and the tall ship's going trim,
And the dark blue skies are paling, and the white stars burning dim;
The long night watch is over, and the long sea-roving done,
And yonder light is the Start Point light, and yonder comes the sun.

O, we have been with the Spaniards, and far and long on the sea;
But there are the twisted chimneys, and the gnarled old inns on the quay.
The wind blows keen as the day breaks, the roofs are white with the rime,
And the church-bells ring as the sun comes up to call men in to Prime.

The church-bells rock and jangle, and there is peace on the earth.
Peace and good will and plenty and Christmas games and mirth.
O, the gold glints bright on the wind-vane as it shifts above the
                                        squire's house,
And the water of the bar of Salcombe is muttering about the bows.

O, the salt sea tide of Salcombe, it wrinkles into wisps of foam,
And the church-bells ring in Salcombe to ring poor sailors home.
The belfry rocks as the bells ring, the chimes are merry as a song,
They ring home wandering sailors who have been homeless long.

The Word

My friend, my bonny friend, when we are old,
And hand in hand go tottering down the hill,
May we be rich in love's refinèd gold,
May love's gold coin be current with us still.

May love be sweeter for the vanished days,
And your most perfect beauty still as dear
As when your troubled singer stood at gaze
In the dear March of a most sacred year.

May what we are be all we might have been,
And that potential, perfect, O my friend,
And may there still be many sheafs to glean
In our love's acre, comrade, till the end.

And may we find when ended is the page
Death but a tavern on our pilgrimage.

from The Street of To-Day

[*'O beauty, I have wandered far...'*]

O beauty, I have wandered far;
Peace, I have suffered seeking thee:
Life, I have sought to see thy star
That other men might see.

And after wandering nights and days,
A gleam in a beloved soul
Shows how life's elemental blaze
Goes wandering through the whole,

Bearing the discipline of earth
That earth, controlled, may bring forth flowers.
O may our labours help the birth
Of nobler souls than ours.

Miscellaneous Verse, 1899–1911

Sonnet – To the Ocean

Though tongues of men and angels both should sing
In tones of wondrous grandeur till their cry
Should rock the roof of Heaven; or, quivering, die
Midst sobs of soul-thrilled peoples listening;
If, from the earth, their glorious chant took wing
And shamed the music of the spheres, to me
The thunder of the never-silent sea,
Ocean's vast chord, would seem more grand a thing.
Not though the Sirens joined the Titans' choir,
Or with Earth's noises the voice of Storm were blent,
Nor if the Earth with some grim throe were rent
Till all void space shook with the breath of fire;
Not even these could shame the Ocean's lyre,
Or still the voice which shakes the firmament.

[written 1896/1897]
[*The Bookman*, Vol. XLVIII, No. 5 (New York: George H. Doran, January 1919), p. 546]

[Before Beginning]

[Written at Tettenhall, Staffs, the night before I left for London to begin life as a writer]

Here by the gipsy fire the dawn breaks bleak and damp
And it's time to scatter the embers and strike and shift the camp
And add more miles to the tally of the grey miles left behind
In the quest of the heart's contentment I'm little like to find.

I have been to the East and the South: I have been to the [North] and
the West
Yet none of the camping places had place for a man to rest.
There's never a road or trackway by which I have not gone
But the blessed town I march to lies always further on.

[Bodleian. Dep.c.314]

Theodore

They sacked the ships of London town,
They burned the ships of Rye and Cadiz,
They pulled full many a city down;
A bloody trade the pirates' trade is.
But Theodore,
Though dripping gore,
Was always courteous to the ladies.

[*A Broad Sheet*, No. 19, July 1903]

['Oh some are fond of cow's milk...']

Oh some are fond of cow's milk and some are fond of gore
And some are fond of sailoring and some are fond of shore
But I am fond of writing of the pyrat Theodore
The cabin-boy to beautiful Constanza.

His brow was white as marble: his blood was white as milk
His nose was like a sunset his close were made of silk
And his talents were in pirating and knowing how to bilk
The pockets of the beautiful Constanza.

His heart was full of virtue: his ways were full of fun
His pickings and his pocketings were very nimbly done
But the quartermaster collared him and tied him to a gun
At the order of the beautiful Constanza.

And first they tried the blood-knot and then they tried the cane
And then they tried the brick-rod and then the cane again
And lastly used the nine-tails till he bellowed with the pain
Of the verdict of the beautiful Constanza.

And then there came the Captain and 'Stop a spell!' says he
'And load him in the carronade and shoot him in the sea
With a wad at either end of him to help him for to be
Dischargéd by the beautiful Constanza.'

They manned the cannon's tacklings: the gunner gave a shout!
And they ran the cannon inboard, and didn't run it out
Till they'd loaded it by ramming skipper Theo up the spout
To the merriment of beautiful Constanza.

And first he felt the cartridge and then he felt the wad
And when he felt the rammer-end he felt a wicked prod.
The gunner down the touch-hole said 'Prepare to meet thy God –
Are you ready Miss?' to beautiful Constanza.

Constanza took the lanyard and the gunner gave a hail
Of 'fire when the blank you like': the trigger didn't fail
And Theo left the cannon like a Jonah from a whale
At the shooting of the beautiful Constanza.

They marked him hit the water, saying, 'That's the end of he!
Now sponge and load the carronade, and let the cannon be.'
And the ship was on her course again a sailing on the sea
With the merry crew of beautiful Constanza.

[Bodleian. MS.Eng.poet.d.194, ff. 16–17]

Theodore to his Mother

No I would not be an office-boy, in a clean and tidy sash,
With never a chance of more than a bob from out of the petty cash.
The days of ruling the scarlet lines, oh beautiful would they be,
But the cash is balanced each Friday night. That isn't the graft for me.

Nor I wouldn't be in a bank, mother; the sight of the brimming till
With its gold doubloons in glittering rolls would certainly make me ill
I should pine away in my youth, mother, my spirit would pine and chafe
At having nought but a single key to a seven-keyed patent safe.

And I wouldn't be 'on the lay', mother, to clutch at the pretty clies
Or make a fake at the Kinchin chit, or cut ben whids with the chyes
The ben rom-bouse in the bousing Ken is well, and better than well,
But the cops are here and the beaks are there, and a stretch in the jug is hell.

I couldn't slug in the ring, mother, or run a joint or a dive,
I'm such a mug with me hands, mother, I'd never come home alive.
I'm as pretty a rogue at heart, mother, as ever put tongue in cheek
I'm black to the chin with sin, mother, its only the flesh is weak.

I'd like to follow the sea, mother, for the sea would wash me clean.
And the sea's wide, and the sea's a place where the laws ain't worth a bean.
Where the green salt water bursts and breaks there's never a cop can come
And a ship's sweet to a nimble lad with a private key to the rum.

So I'm off away to the sea, mother. It's sorry I am to leave.
But the sea calls, and the wind calls, and the rope's in the creaking sheave.
You'll pray for me in the nights, mother, 'that the angels of grace defend
Your only son from the shot, mother, and the dangling noose's end.'

[Bodleian. MS.Eng.poet.d.194, f. 6]

Vallipo

The maids in pleasant Vallipo have bonny black hair,
And delicate sweet faces, and tremulous lips,
And golden-twisted ear-rings, and the subtle Spanish air
As they walk among the sailors on the slips.

The bells that ring at Vallipo are soft and sleepy-sweet
As they chime above the gardens where the lilies grow,
And when the sailors' lamps are lit it's good to walk the street
While the gentle bells aloft chime slow.

The ships that lie at Vallipo are decked with scented wood,
And bales of purple tissue is the freight they bring,
And sticks of scarlet coral, and the green gems good
From the grave-mound of an Indian king.

O Vallipo's a sweet town, the blossom of the earth,
A town of marble houses by the dim blue seas;
And o' nights the sailors sing there, while the maids make mirth,
And the pale moon tops the orange trees.

[*The Manchester Guardian*, 14 November 1904, p. 5]

The Gara Brook

Babbling and rippling as over the pebbles it bubbles
Slips the cold brook from the dripping wet woods to the piers,
Passing the acres in stook and the dull yellow stalks of the stubbles,
On to the sea and the ships and the sailors with rings in their ears.

Over the tremulous grasses it gurgles and gushes,
Leaving the fields that are sweet with the smell of the fruit,
Lapping the hooves of the kine and the green, rusty bunches of rushes,
Washing the heavy red clay from the twists of the alder-tree root.

Babbling and rippling, it sings past the bend, past the boulders,
On to the sea and the ships and the songs of the men on the quay–
Men who are tanned in the cheeks and strong in the arms and the shoulders,
Men with the swaggering walk and the tarry, salt ways of the sea.

Would I could follow the brook to the pier where the schooners are lying,
Drying brown sails in the sun, while the mariners drink at the inn;
Would I could drift with the stream to the bay where the gannets are crying,
There where the shore dies away and the merry adventures begin.

[*The Manchester Guardian*, 18 November 1904, p. 5]

Westward Ho

The wind smells of heather and the white-blossomed may;
It blew down the brown hills, down to the bay;
It sings in the rigging, it sings in the sky;
It shakes the green waves and makes the salt spray fly.

The white clouds are scattering – it blows half a gale;
So break out the anchor and shake out the sail,
And sheet home the topsail and let the hooker go,
Through the grey gull's fishery and westward ho.

And we will come to anchor in a bay of blue calm,
Where the parrots scream and clatter in the green-plumed palm;
Where the galley and the galleon, the brig and brigantine,
From sailing Spanish waters, come in to careen.

And there will be the sunshine and the thronged sea piers,
And merry taverns full of the tarry buccaneers,
And jolly sailors dancing, and songs for our delight,
And Spanish wine and sweet wine, and red wine and white.

[*The Manchester Guardian*, 26 November 1904, p. 7]

The Whale

[Adapted by John Masefield]

It was in the year of ninety-four, in March the twentieth day,
Our gallant tars their anchors weigh'd, and for sea they bore away,
Brave boys,
And for sea they bore away.

Speedicut was our captain's name, our ship was the *Lyon* bold,
And we have gone to sea, brave boys, to face the storm and cold,
To face the storm and the cold.

When that we came to the cold country where the frost and the snow
                                                        did lie,
Where the frost, and the snow, and the whale-fish so blue, and the
                                                        daylight's never gone,
Brave boys,
And the daylight's never gone.

Our boatswain went to topmast high, with his spy-glass in his hand,
'A whale, a whale, a whale,' he did cry, 'and she blows at every span,
Brave boys,
She blows at every span.'

Our captain stood on the quarter-deck, and a clever little man was he,
'Overhaul, overhaul, let the wind-tackle fall, and to launch your boats
so free,
Brave boys,
And to launch your boats so free!'

There's harpooneers, and line coilers, and line[1] colecks also,
There's boat-steerers and sailors brave,
To the whale, to where she blows, to the whale, to where she blows,
Brave boys,
To the whale, to where she blows.

We struck the whale, and away she went, casts a flourish with her tail,
But, Oh, and alas, we've lost one man, and we did not kill that whale
Brave boys,
And we did not kill that whale.

When that the news to our captain it did come, a sorrowful man was he,
For the losing of his prentice boy, and down his colours drew he,
Brave boys
And down his colours drew he.

Now, my lads, don't be amazed for the losing of one man;
For fortune it will take its place, let a man do all he can,
Brave boys,
Let a man do all he can.

1. So in my original.

[*A Sailor's Garland* (London: Methuen & Co., 1906), pp. 178–80]

The Salcombe Seaman's Flaunt to the Proud Pirate

A lofty ship from Salcombe came,
Blow high, blow low, and so sailed we;
She had golden trucks that shone like flame,
On the bonny coasts of Barbary.

'Masthead, masthead,' the captains hail,
Blow high, blow low, and so sailed we;
'Look out and round; d'ye see a sail?'
On the bonny coasts of Barbary.

'There's a ship what looms like Beachy Head,'
Blow high, blow low, and so sailed we;
'Her banner aloft it blows out red,'
On the bonny coasts of Barbary.

'Oh, ship ahoy, and where do you steer?'
Blow high, blow low, and so sailed we;
'Are you man-of-war, or privateer?'
On the bonny coasts of Barbary.

'I am neither one of the two,' said she,
Blow high, blow low, and so sailed we;
'I'm a pirate, looking for my fee,'
On the bonny coasts of Barbary.

'I'm a jolly pirate, out for gold:'
Blow high, blow low, and so sailed we;
'I will rummage through your after hold,'
On the bonny coasts of Barbary.

The grumbling guns they flashed and roared,
Blow high, blow low, and so sailed we;
Till the pirate's masts went overboard,
On the bonny coasts of Barbary.

They fired shot till the pirate's deck,
Blow high, blow low, and so sailed we;
Was blood and spars and broken wreck,
On the bonny coasts of Barbary.

'O do not haul the red flag down,'
Blow high, blow low, and so sailed we;
'O keep all fast until we drown,'
On the bonny coasts of Barbary.

They called for cans of wine, and drank,
Blow high, blow low, and so sailed we;
They sang their songs until she sank,
On the bonny coasts of Barbary.

Now let us brew good cans of flip,
Blow high, blow low, and so sailed we;
And drink a bowl to the Salcombe ship,
On the bonny coasts of Barbary.

And drink a bowl to the lad of fame,
Blow high, blow low, and so sailed we;
Who put the pirate ship to shame,
On the bonny coasts of Barbary.

[*A Sailor's Garland* (London: Methuen & Co., 1906), pp. 293–4]

Campeachy Picture

The sloop's sails glow in the sun; the far sky burns,
Over the palm tree tops wanders the dusk,
About the bows a chuckling ripple churns;
The land wind from the marshes smells of musk.
A star comes out: the moon is a pale husk;
Now, from the galley door, as supper nears,
Comes a sharp scent of meat and Spanish rusk
Fried in a pan. Far aft, where the lamp blears,
A seaman in a red shirt eyes the sails and steers.

Soon he will sight that isle in the dim bay
Where his mates saunter by the camp-fire's glow;
Soon will the birds scream, scared, and the bucks bray,
At the rattle and splash as the anchor is let go:
A block will pipe, and the oars grunt as they row,
He will meet his friends beneath the shadowy trees,
The moon's orb like a large lamp hanging low
Will see him stretched by the red blaze at ease,
Telling of the Indian girls, of ships, and of the seas.

[*A Broadside*, No. 1 (Dundrum, Co. Dublin: Dun Emer Press, June
1908), pp.1–2]

Theodore to his Grandson

Grandson   O gamfer: you are lined and old,
Your nose is blue, your hands are cold,
Your wrinkles twist and groove and fold,
Your withered spine is bending.

O tell this child, this little lad,
What you were like when you were bad,
And what defence you could have had
Could aught deserve defending?

Theodore   Why as to that, my little son,
Blood spilt is spilt, man dead is done,
We took and blowed em from a gun,
Or sawed em in halves, sir.

And rum, red rum, is my delight,
It makes my old hulk watertight;
Or give me two dogs to set to fight
Tradoodle.

[*A Broadside*, No. 8 (Dundrum, Co. Dublin: Cuala Press, January
1909), p. 1]

By a Bier-Side

This is a sacred city built of marvellous earth.
Life was lived nobly here to give such beauty birth.
Beauty was in this brain and in this eager hand;
Death is so blind and dumb Death does not understand.
Death drifts the brain with dust and soils the young limbs' glory
Death makes justice a dream, and strength a traveller's story
Death drives the lovely soul to wander under the sky
Death opens unknown doors. It is most grand to die.

[*The Englishwoman*, No. 3, April 1909, p. 236]

Chorus

Kneel to the beautiful women who bear us this strange brave fruit,
Man with his soul so noble, man half god and half brute.
Women bear him in pain that he may bring them tears,
He is a King on earth, he rules for a term of years.
And the conqueror's prize is dust, and lost endeavour.
And the beaten man becomes a story for ever.
For the gods employ strange means to bring their will to be;
We are in the wise gods' hands, and more we cannot see.

[*The Englishwoman*, No. 7, August 1909, p. 41]

[The Pirate Poet on the Monte*]*

And now by Gara rushes,
When stars are blinking white;
And sleep has stilled the thrushes,
And sunset brings the night;

There, where the stones are gleamin',
A passer-by can hark
To the old drowned *Monte* seamen
A-singing through the dark.

There, where the gnats are pesky,
They sing like anything;
They sing like Jean de Reszke,
This is the song they sing:

Down in the pebbled ridges
Our old bones sing and shout;
We see the dancing midges,
We feel the skipping trout.

Our bones are green and weeded,
Our bones are old and wet;
But the noble deeds that we did
We never can forget.

[Jack B. Yeats, *A Little Fleet* (London: Elkin Mathews [1909]), pp. 9–10]

from The Everlasting Mercy

Saul Kane's Madness

I opened window wide and leaned
Out of that pigstye of the fiend
And felt a cool wind go like grace
About the sleeping market-place.
The clock struck three, and sweetly, slowly,
The bells chimed Holy, Holy, Holy;
And in a second's pause there fell
The cold note of the chapel bell,
And then a cock crew, flapping wings,
And summat made me think of things.
How long those ticking clocks had gone
From church and chapel, on and on,
Ticking the time out, ticking slow
To men and girls who'd come and go,
And how they ticked in belfry dark
When half the town was bishop's park,
And how they'd rung a chime full tilt
The night after the church was built,
And how that night was Lambert's Feast,
The night I'd fought and been a beast.
And how a change had come. And then
I thought, 'You tick to different men.'

What with the fight and what with drinking
And being awake alone there thinking,
My mind began to carp and tetter,
'If this life's all, the beasts are better.'
And then I thought, 'I wish I'd seen
The many towns this town has been;
I wish I knew if they'd a-got
A kind of summat we've a-not,
If them as built the church so fair

Were half the chaps folk say they were;
For they'd the skill to draw their plan,
And skill's a joy to any man;
And they'd the strength, not skill alone,
To build it beautiful in stone;
And strength and skill together thus
O, they were happier men than us.

But if they were, they had to die
The same as every one and I.
And no one lives again, but dies,
And all the bright goes out of eyes,
And all the skill goes out of hands,
And all the wise brain understands,
And all the beauty, all the power
Is cut down like a withered flower.
In all the show from birth to rest
I give the poor dumb cattle best.'

I wondered, then, why life should be,
And what would be the end of me
When youth and health and strength were gone
And cold old age came creeping on?
A keeper's gun? The Union ward?
Or that new quod at Hereford?
And looking round I felt disgust
At all the nights of drink and lust,
And all the looks of all the swine
Who'd said that they were friends of mine;
And yet I knew, when morning came,
The morning would be just the same,
For I'd have drinks and Jane would meet me
And drunken Silas Jones would greet me,
And I'd risk quod and keeper's gun
Till all the silly game was done.
'For parson chaps are mad, supposin'
A chap can change the road he's chosen.'
And then the Devil whispered, 'Saul,
Why should you want to live at all?
Why fret and sweat and try to mend?
It's all the same thing in the end.

But when it's done,' he said, 'its ended.
Why stand it, since it can't be mended?'
And in my heart I heard him plain,
'Throw yourself down and end it, Kane.'

'Why not?' said I. 'Why not? But no.
I won't. I've never had my go.
I've not had all the world can give.
Death by and by, but first I'll live.
The world owes me my time of times,
And that time's coming now, by crimes.'

A madness took me then. I felt
I'd like to hit the world a belt.
I felt that I could fly through air,
A screaming star with blazing hair,
A rushing comet, crackling, numbing
The folk with fear of judgment coming,
A 'Lijah in a fiery car
Coming to tell folk what they are.

'That's what I'll do,' I shouted loud,
'I'll tell this sanctimonious crowd
This town of window peeping, prying,
Maligning, peering, hinting, lying,
Male and female human blots
Who would, but daren't be, whores and sots,
That they're so steeped in petty vice
That they're less excellent than lice,
That they're so soaked in petty virtue
That touching one of them will dirt you,
Dirt you with the stain of mean
Cheating trade and going between,
Pinching, starving, scraping, hoarding,
Spying through the chinks of boarding
To see if Sue the prentice lean
Dares to touch the margarine.
Fawning, cringing, oiling boots,
Raging in the crowd's pursuits,
Flinging stones at all the Stephens,
Standing firm with all the evens,

Making hell for all the odd,
All the lonely ones of God,
Those poor lonely ones who find
Dogs more mild than human kind.
For dogs,' I said, 'are nobles born
To most of you, you cockled corn.
I've known dogs to leave their dinner,
Nosing a kind heart in a sinner.
Poor old Crafty wagged his tail
The day I first came home from jail,
When all my folk, so primly clad,
Glowered black and thought me mad,
And muttered how they'd been respected,
While I was what they'd all expected.
(I've thought of that old dog for years,
And of how near I come to tears.)

But you, you minds of bread and cheese,
Are less divine than that dog's fleas.
You suck blood from kindly friends,
And kill them when it serves your ends.
Double traitors, double black,
Stabbing only in the back,
Stabbing with the knives you borrow
From the friends you bring to sorrow.
You stab all that's true and strong,
Truth and strength you say are wrong,
Meek and mild, and sweet and creeping,
Repeating, canting, cadging, peeping,
That's the art and that's the life
To win a man his neighbour's wife.
All that's good and all that's true,
You kill that, so I'll kill you.'

At that I tore my clothes in shreds
And hurled them on the window leads;
I flung my boots through both the winders
And knocked the glass to little flinders;
The punch bowl and the tumblers followed,
And then I seized the lamps and holloed,
And down the stairs, and tore back bolts,

57

As mad as twenty blooded colts;
And out into the street I pass,
As mad as two-year-olds at grass,
A naked madman waving grand
A blazing lamp in either hand.
I yelled like twenty drunken sailors,
'The devil's come among the tailors.'
A blaze of flame behind me streamed,
And then I clashed the lamps and screamed
'I'm Satan, newly come from hell.'
And then I spied the fire bell.

I've been a ringer, so I know
How best to make a big bell go.
So on to bell-rope swift I swoop,
And stick my one foot in the loop
And heave a down-swig till I groan,
'Awake, you swine, you devil's own.'

I made the fire-bell awake,
I felt the bell-rope throb and shake;
I felt the air mingle and clang
And beat the walls a muffled bang,
And stifle back and boom and bay
Like muffled peals on Boxing Day,
And then surge up and gather shape,
And spread great pinions and escape;
And each great bird of clanging shrieks
O Fire! Fire, from iron beaks.
My shoulders cracked to send around
Those shrieking birds made out of sound
With news of fire in their bills.
(They heard 'em plain beyond Wall Hills.)

Up go the winders, out come heads,
I heard the springs go creak in beds;
But still I heave and sweat and tire,
And still the clang goes 'Fire, Fire!'
'Where is it, then? Who is it, there?
You ringer, stop, and tell us where.'
'Run round and let the Captain know.'

'It must be bad, he's ringing so.'
'It's in the town, I see the flame;
Look there! Look there, how red it came.'
'Where is it, then? O stop the bell.'
I stopped and called: 'It's fire of hell;
And this is Sodom and Gomorrah,
And now I'll burn you up, begorra.'

By this the firemen were mustering,
The half-dressed stable men were flustering,
Backing the horses out of stalls
While this man swears and that man bawls,
'Don't take th' old mare. Back, Toby, back.
Back, Lincoln. Where's the fire, Jack?'
'Damned if I know. Out Preston way.'
'No. It's at Chancey's Pitch, they say.'
'It's sixteen ricks at Pauntley burnt.'
'You back old Darby out, I durn't.'
They ran the big red engine out,
And put 'em to with damn and shout.
And then they start to raise the shire,
'Who brought the news, and where's the fire?'
They'd moonlight, lamps, and gas to light 'em.
I give a screech-owl's screech to fright 'em,
And snatch from underneath their noses
The nozzles of the fire hoses.
'I am the fire. Back, stand back,
Or else I'll fetch your skulls a crack;
D'you see these copper nozzles here?
They weigh ten pounds apiece, my dear;
I'm fire of hell come up this minute
To burn this town, and all that's in it.
To burn you dead and burn you clean,
You cogwheels in a stopped machine,
You hearts of snakes, and brains of pigeons,
You dead devout of dead religions,
You offspring of the hen and ass,
By Pilate ruled, and Caiaphas.
Now your account is totted. Learn
Hell's flames are loose and you shall burn.'

At that I leaped and screamed and ran,
I heard their cries go 'Catch him, man.'
'Who was it?' 'Down him.' 'Out him, Ern.'
'Duck him at pump, we'll see who'll burn.'
A policeman clutched, a fireman clutched,
A dozen others snatched and touched.
'By God, he's stripped down to his buff.'
'By God, we'll make him warm enough.'
'After him.' 'Catch him,' 'Out him,' 'Scrob him.'
'We'll give him hell.' 'By God, we'll mob him.'
'We'll duck him, scrout him, flog him, fratch him.'
'All right,' I said. 'But first you'll catch him.'

['O lovely lily clean…']

O lovely lily clean,
O lily springing green,
O lily bursting white,
Dear lily of delight,
Spring in my heart agen
That I may flower to men.

from The Widow in the Bye Street

[The Ending]

And sometimes she will walk the cindery mile,
Singing, as she and Jimmy used to do,
Singing 'The parson's dog lep over a stile,'
Along the path where water lilies grew.
The stars are placid on the evening's blue,
Burning like eyes so calm, so unafraid,
On all that God has given and man has made.

Burning they watch, and mothlike owls come out,
The redbreast warbles shrilly once and stops;
The homing cowman gives his dog a shout,
The lamps are lighted in the village shops.
Silence; the last bird passes; in the copse
The hazels cross the moon, a nightjar spins,
Dew wets the grass, the nightingale begins.

Singing her crazy song the mother goes,
Singing as though her heart were full of peace,
Moths knock the petals from the dropping rose,
Stars make the glimmering pool a golden fleece,
The moon droops west, but still she does not cease,
The little mice peep out to hear her sing,
Until the inn-man's cockerel shakes his wing.

And in the sunny dawns of hot Julys,
The labourers going to meadow see her there.
Rubbing the sleep out of their heavy eyes,
They lean upon the parapet to stare;
They see her plaiting basil in her hair,
Basil, the dark red wound-wort, cops of clover,
The blue self-heal and golden Jacks of Dover.

Dully they watch her, then they turn to go
To that high Shropshire upland of late hay;
Her singing lingers with them as they mow,
And many times they try it, now grave, now gay,
Till, with full throat, over the hills away,
They lift it clear; oh, very clear it towers
Mixed with the swish of many falling flowers.

from Dauber

[*'Denser it grew…'*]

Denser it grew, until the ship was lost.
The elemental hid her; she was merged
In mufflings of dark death, like a man's ghost,
New to the change of death, yet thither urged.
Then from the hidden waters something surged –
Mournful, despairing, great, greater than speech,
A noise like one slow wave on a still beach.

Mournful, and then again mournful, and still
Out of the night that mighty voice arose;
The Dauber at his foghorn felt the thrill.
Who rode that desolate sea? What forms were those?
Mournful, from things defeated, in the throes
Of memory of some conquered hunting-ground,
Out of the night of death arose the sound.

'Whales!' said the mate. They stayed there all night long
Answering the horn. Out of the night they spoke,
Defeated creatures who had suffered wrong,
But were still noble underneath the stroke.
They filled the darkness when the Dauber woke;
The men came peering to the rail to hear,
And the sea sighed, and the fog rose up sheer.

A wall of nothing at the world's last edge,
Where no life came except defeated life.
The Dauber felt shut in within a hedge,
Behind which form was hidden and thought was rife,
And that a blinding flash, a thrust, a knife
Would sweep the hedge away and make all plain,
Brilliant beyond all words, blinding the brain.

So the night past, but then no morning broke –
Only a something showed that night was dead.
A sea-bird, cackling like a devil, spoke,
And the fog drew away and hung like lead.
Like mighty cliffs it shaped, sullen and red;
Like glowering gods at watch it did appear,
And sometimes drew away, and then drew near.

Like islands, and like chasms, and like hell,
But always mighty and red, gloomy and ruddy,
Shutting the visible sea in like a well;
Slow heaving in vast ripples, blank and muddy,
Where the sun should have risen it streaked bloody.
The day was still-born; all the sea-fowl scattering
Splashed the still water, mewing, hovering, clattering.

Then Polar snow came down little and light,
Till all the sky was hidden by the small,
Most multitudinous drift of dirty white
Tumbling and wavering down and covering all –
Covering the sky, the sea, the clipper tall,
Furring the ropes with white, casing the mast,
Coming on no known air, but blowing past.

And all the air seemed full of gradual moan,
As though in those cloud-chasms the horns were blowing
The mort for gods cast out and overthrown,
Or for the eyeless sun plucked out and going.
Slow the low gradual moan came in the snowing;
The Dauber felt the prelude had begun.
The snowstorm fluttered by; he saw the sun

Show and pass by, gleam from one towering prison
Into another, vaster and more grim,
Which in dull crags of darkness had arisen
To muffle-to a final door on him.
The gods upon the dull crags lowered dim,
The pigeons chattered, quarrelling in the track.
In the south-west the dimness dulled to black.

Then came the cry of 'Call all hands on deck!'
The Dauber knew its meaning; it was come:
Cape Horn, that tramples beauty into wreck,
And crumples steel and smites the strong man dumb.
Down clattered flying kites and staysails: some
Sang out in quick, high calls; the fairleads skirled,
And from the south-west came the end of the world.

We Therefore Commit Our Brother

Night fell, and all night long the Dauber lay
Covered upon the table; all night long
The pitiless storm exulted at her prey,
Huddling the waters with her icy thong.
But to the covered shape she did no wrong.
He lay beneath the sailcloth. Bell by bell
The night wore through; the stars rose, the stars fell.

Blowing most pitiless cold out of clear sky
The wind roared all night long; and all night through
The green seas on the deck went washing by,
Flooding the half-deck; bitter hard it blew.
But little of it all the Dauber knew –
The sopping bunks, the floating chests, the wet,
The darkness, and the misery, and the sweat.

He was off duty. So it blew all night,
And when the watches changed the men would come
Dripping within the door to strike a light
And stare upon the Dauber lying dumb,
And say, 'He come a cruel thump, poor chum.'
Or, 'He'd a-been a fine big man;' or, 'He...
A smart young seaman he was getting to be.'

Or, 'Damn it all, it's what we've all to face!...
I knew another fellow one time...' then
Came a strange tale of death in a strange place
Out on the sea, in ships, with wandering men.
In many ways Death puts us into pen.
The reefers came down tired and looked and slept.
Below the skylight little dribbles crept

Along the painted woodwork, glistening, slow,
Following the roll and dripping, never fast,
But dripping on the quiet form below,
Like passing time talking to time long past.
And all night long 'Ai, ai!' went the wind's blast,
And creaming water swished below the pale,
Unheeding body stretched beneath the sail.

At dawn they sewed him up, and at eight bells
They bore him to the gangway, wading deep,
Through the green-clutching, white-toothed water-hells
That flung his carriers over in their sweep.
They laid an old red ensign on the heap,
And all hands stood bare-headed, stooping, swaying,
Washed by the sea while the old man was praying

Out of a borrowed prayer-book. At a sign
They twitched the ensign back and tipped the grating
A creamier bubbling broke the bubbling brine.
The muffled figure tilted to the weighting;
It dwindled slowly down, slowly gyrating.
Some craned to see; it dimmed, it disappeared;
The last green milky bubble blinked and cleared.

'Mister, shake out your reefs,' the Captain called.
'Out topsail reefs!' the Mate cried; then all hands
Hurried, the great sails shook, and all hands hauled,
Singing that desolate song of lonely lands,
Of how a lover came in dripping bands,
Green with the wet and cold, to tell his lover
That Death was in the sea, and all was over.

Fair came the falling wind; a seaman said
The Dauber was a Jonah; once again
The clipper held her course, showing red lead,
Shattering the sea-tops into golden rain.
The waves bowed down before her like blown grain;
Onwards she thundered, on; her voyage was short,
Before the tier's bells rang her into port.

Cheerly they rang her in, those beating bells,
The new-come beauty stately from the sea,
Whitening the blue heave of the drowsy swells,
Treading the bubbles down. With three times three
They cheered her moving beauty in, and she
Came to her berth so noble, so superb;
Swayed like a queen, and answered to the curb.

Then in the sunset's flush they went aloft,
And unbent sails in that most lovely hour,
When the light gentles and the wind is soft,
And beauty in the heart breaks like a flower.
Working aloft they saw the mountain tower,
Snow to the peak; they heard the launchmen shout;
And bright along the bay the lights came out.

And then the night fell dark, and all night long
The pointed mountain pointed at the stars,
Frozen, alert, austere; the eagle's song
Screamed from her desolate screes and splintered scars.
On her intense crags where the air is sparse
The stars looked down; their many golden eyes
Watched her and burned, burned out, and came to rise.

Silent the finger of the summit stood,
Icy in pure, thin air, glittering with snows.
Then the sun's coming turned the peak to blood,
And in the rest-house the muleteers arose.
And all day long, where only the eagle goes,
Stones, loosened by the sun, fall; the stones falling
Fill empty gorge on gorge with echoes calling.

from Philip the King and other poems

Truth

Man with his burning soul
Has but an hour of breath
To build a ship of truth
In which his soul may sail –
Sail on the sea of death,
For death takes toll
Of beauty, courage, youth,
Of all but truth.

Life's city ways are dark,
Men mutter by; the wells
Of the great waters moan.
O death! O sea! O tide!
The waters moan like bells;
No light, no mark,
The soul goes out alone
On seas unknown.

Stripped of all purple robes,
Stripped of all golden lies,
I will not be afraid,
Truth will preserve through death.
Perhaps the stars will rise –
The stars like globes;
The ship my striving made
May see night fade.

The Wanderer

All day they loitered by the resting ships,
Telling their beauties over, taking stock;
At night the verdict left my messmates' lips,
'The *Wanderer* is the finest ship in dock.'

I had not seen her, but a friend, since drowned,
Drew her, with painted ports, low, lovely, lean,
Saying, 'The *Wanderer*, clipper, outward bound,
The loveliest ship my eyes have ever seen –

Perhaps to-morrow you will see her sail.
She sails at sunrise': but the morrow showed
No *Wanderer* setting forth for me to hail;
Far down the stream men pointed where she rode,

Rode the great trackway to the sea, dim, dim,
Already gone before the stars were gone.
I saw her at the sea-line's smoky rim
Grow swiftly vaguer as they towed her on.

Soon even her masts were hidden in the haze
Beyond the city; she was on her course
To trample billows for a hundred days;
That afternoon the norther gathered force,

Blowing a small snow from a point of east.
'Oh, fair for her,' we said, 'to take her south.'
And in our spirits, as the wind increased,
We saw her there, beyond the river mouth,

Setting her side-lights in the wildering dark,
To glint upon mad water, while the gale
Roared like a battle, snapping like a shark,
And drunken seamen struggled with the sail.

While with sick hearts her mates put out of mind
Their little children left astern, ashore,
And the gale's gathering made the darkness blind,
Water and air one intermingled roar.

Then we forgot her, for the fiddlers played,
Dancing and singing held our merry crew;
The old ship moaned a little as she swayed.
It blew all night, oh, bitter hard it blew!

So that at midnight I was called on deck
To keep an anchor-watch: I heard the sea
Roar past in white procession filled with wreck;
Intense bright frosty stars burned over me,

And the Greek brig beside us dipped and dipped,
White to the muzzle like a half-tide rock,
Drowned to the mainmast with the seas she shipped;
Her cable-swivels clanged at every shock.

And like a never-dying force, the wind
Roared till we shouted with it, roared until
Its vast vitality of wrath was thinned,
Had beat its fury breathless and was still.

By dawn the gale had dwindled into flaw,
A glorious morning followed: with my friend
I climbed the fo'c's'le-head to see; we saw
The waters hurrying shorewards without end.

Haze blotted out the river's lowest reach;
Out of the gloom the steamers, passing by,
Called with their sirens, hooting their sea-speech;
Out of the dimness others made reply.

And as we watched, there came a rush of feet
Charging the fo'c's'le till the hatchway shook.
Men all about us thrust their way, or beat,
Crying, 'The *Wanderer*! Down the river! Look!'

I looked with them towards the dimness; there
Gleamed like a spirit striding out of night,
A full-rigged ship unutterably fair,
Her masts like trees in winter, frosty-bright.

Foam trembled at her bows like wisps of wool;
She trembled as she towed. I had not dreamed
That work of man could be so beautiful,
In its own presence and in what it seemed.

'So, she is putting back again,' I said.
'How white with frost her yards are on the fore.'
One of the men about me answer made,
'That is not frost, but all her sails are tore,

Torn into tatters, youngster, in the gale;
Her best foul-weather suit gone.' It was true,
Her masts were white with rags of tattered sail
Many as gannets when the fish are due.

Beauty in desolation was her pride,
Her crowned array a glory that had been;
She faltered tow'rds us like a swan that died,
But although ruined she was still a queen.

'Put back with all her sails gone,' went the word;
Then, from her signals flying, rumour ran,
'The sea that stove her boats in killed her third;
She has been gutted and has lost a man.'

So, as though stepping to a funeral march,
She passed defeated homewards whence she came
Ragged with tattered canvas white as starch,
A wild bird that misfortune had made tame.

She was refitted soon: another took
The dead man's office; then the singers hove
Her capstan till the snapping hawsers shook;
Out, with a bubble at her bows, she drove.

Again they towed her seawards, and again
We, watching, praised her beauty, praised her trim,
Saw her fair house-flag flutter at the main,
And slowly saunter seawards, dwindling dim;

And wished her well, and wondered, as she died,
How, when her canvas had been sheeted home,
Her quivering length would sweep into her stride,
Making the greenness milky with her foam.

But when we rose next morning, we discerned
Her beauty once again a shattered thing;
Towing to dock the *Wanderer* returned,
A wounded sea-bird with a broken wing.

A spar was gone, her rigging's disarray
Told of a worse disaster than the last;
Like draggled hair dishevelled hung the stay,
Drooping and beating on the broken mast.

Half-mast upon her flagstaff hung her flag;
Word went among us how the broken spar
Had gored her captain like an angry stag,
And killed her mate a half-day from the bar.

She passed to dock upon the top of flood.
An old man near me shook his head and swore:
'Like a bad woman, she has tasted blood –
There'll be no trusting in her any more.'

We thought it truth, and when we saw her there
Lying in dock, beyond, across the stream,
We would forget that we had called her fair,
We thought her murderess and the past a dream.

And when she sailed again, we watched in awe,
Wondering what bloody act her beauty planned,
What evil lurked behind the thing we saw,
What strength was there that thus annulled man's hand,

How next its triumph would compel man's will
Into compliance with external Fate,
How next the powers would use her to work ill
On suffering men; we had not long to wait.

For soon the outcry of derision rose,
'Here comes the *Wanderer*!' the expected cry.
Guessing the cause, our mockings joined with those
Yelled from the shipping as they towed her by.

She passed us close, her seamen paid no heed
To what was called: they stood, a sullen group,
Smoking and spitting, careless of her need,
Mocking the orders given from the poop.

Her mates and boys were working her; we stared.
What was the reason of this strange return,
This third annulling of the thing prepared?
No outward evil could our eyes discern.

Only like one who having formed a plan
Beyond the pitch of common minds, she sailed,
Mocked and deserted by the common man,
Made half divine to me for having failed.

We learned the reason soon; below the town
A stay had parted like a snapping reed,
'Warning,' the men thought, 'not to take her down.'
They took the omen, they would not proceed.

Days passed before another crew would sign.
The *Wanderer* lay in dock alone, unmanned,
Feared as a thing possessed by powers malign,
Bound under curses not to leave the land.

But under passing Time fear passes too;
That terror passed, the sailors' hearts grew bold.
We learned in time that she had found a crew
And was bound out and southwards as of old.

And in contempt we thought, 'A little while
Will bring her back again, dismantled, spoiled.
It is herself; she cannot change her style;
She has the habit now of being foiled.'

So when a ship appeared among the haze,
We thought, 'The *Wanderer* back again'; but no,
No *Wanderer* showed for many, many days,
Her passing lights made other waters glow.

But we would often think and talk of her,
Tell newer hands her story, wondering, then,
Upon what ocean she was *Wanderer*,
Bound to the cities built by foreign men.

And one by one our little conclave thinned,
Passed into ships and sailed and so away,
To drown in some great roaring of the wind,
Wanderers themselves, unhappy fortune's prey.

And Time went by me making memory dim,
Yet still I wondered if the *Wanderer* fared
Still pointing to the unreached ocean's rim,
Brightening the water where her breast was bared.

And much in ports abroad I eyed the ships,
Hoping to see her well-remembered form
Come with a curl of bubbles at her lips
Bright to her berth, the sovereign of the storm.

I never did, and many years went by,
Then, near a Southern port, one Christmas Eve,
I watched a gale go roaring through the sky,
Making the caldrons of the clouds upheave.

Then the wrack tattered and the stars appeared,
Millions of stars that seemed to speak in fire;
A byre cock cried aloud that morning neared,
The swinging wind-vane flashed upon the spire.

And soon men looked upon a glittering earth,
Intensely sparkling like a world new-born;
Only to look was spiritual birth,
So bright the raindrops ran along the thorn.

So bright they were, that one could almost pass
Beyond their twinkling to the source, and know
The glory pushing in the blade of grass,
That hidden soul which makes the flowers grow.

That soul was there apparent, not revealed,
Unearthly meanings covered every tree,
That wet grass grew in an immortal field,
Those waters fed some never-wrinkled sea.

The scarlet berries in the hedge stood out
Like revelations but the tongue unknown;
Even in the brooks a joy was quick: the trout
Rushed in a dumbness dumb to me alone.

All of the valley was aloud with brooks;
I walked the morning, breasting up the fells,
Taking again lost childhood from the rooks,
Whose cawing came above the Christmas bells.

I had not walked that glittering world before,
But up the hill a prompting came to me,
'This line of upland runs along the shore:
Beyond the hedgerow I shall see the sea.'

And on the instant from beyond away
That long familiar sound, a ship's bell, broke
The hush below me in the unseen bay.
Old memories came: that inner prompting spoke.

And bright above the hedge a seagull's wings
Flashed and were steady upon empty air.
'A Power unseen,' I cried, 'prepares these things;
Those are her bells, the *Wanderer* is there.'

So, hurrying to the hedge and looking down,
I saw a mighty bay's wind-crinkled blue
Ruffling the image of a tranquil town,
With lapsing waters glittering as they grew.

And near me in the road the shipping swung,
So stately and so still in such great peace
That like to drooping crests their colours hung,
Only their shadows trembled without cease.

I did but glance upon those anchored ships.
Even as my thought had told, I saw her plain;
Tense, like a supple athlete with lean hips,
Swiftness at pause, the *Wanderer* come again –

Come as of old a queen, untouched by Time,
Resting the beauty that no seas could tire,
Sparkling, as though the midnight's rain were rime,
Like a man's thought transfigured into fire.

And as I looked, one of her men began
To sing some simple tune of Christmas day;
Among her crew the song spread, man to man,
Until the singing rang across the bay;

And soon in other anchored ships the men
Joined in the singing with clear throats, until
The farm-boy heard it up the windy glen,
Above the noise of sheep-bells on the hill.

Over the water came the lifted song –
Blind pieces in a mighty game we swing;
Life's battle is a conquest for the strong;
The meaning shows in the defeated thing.

August, 1914

How still this quiet cornfield is to-night!
By an intenser glow the evening falls,
Bringing, not darkness, but a deeper light;
Among the stooks a partridge covey calls.

The windows glitter on the distant hill;
Beyond the hedge the sheep-bells in the fold
Stumble on sudden music and are still;
The forlorn pinewoods droop above the wold.

An endless quiet valley reaches out
Past the blue hills into the evening sky;
Over the stubble, cawing, goes a rout
Of rooks from harvest, flagging as they fly.

So beautiful it is, I never saw
So great a beauty on these English fields,
Touched by the twilight's coming into awe,
Ripe to the soul and rich with summer's yields.

*   *   *   *

These homes, this valley spread below me here,
The rooks, the tilted stacks, the beasts in pen,
Have been the heartfelt things, past-speaking dear
To unknown generations of dead men,

Who, century after century, held these farms,
And, looking out to watch the changing sky,
Heard, as we hear, the rumours and alarms
Of war at hand and danger pressing nigh.

And knew, as we know, that the message meant
The breaking off of ties, the loss of friends,
Death, like a miser getting in his rent,
And no new stones laid where the trackway ends.

The harvest not yet won, the empty bin,
The friendly horses taken from the stalls,
The fallow on the hill not yet brought in,
The cracks unplastered in the leaking walls.

Yet heard the news, and went discouraged home,
And brooded by the fire with heavy mind,
With such dumb loving of the Berkshire loam
As breaks the dumb hearts of the English kind,

Then sadly rose and left the well-loved Downs,
And so by ship to sea, and knew no more
The fields of home, the byres, the market towns,
Nor the dear outline of the English shore,

But knew the misery of the soaking trench,
The freezing in the rigging, the despair
In the revolting second of the wrench
When the blind soul is flung against the air,

And died (uncouthly, most) in foreign lands
For some idea but dimly understood
Of an English city never built by hands
Which love of England prompted and made good.

*   *   *   *

If there be any life beyond the grave,
It must be near the men and things we love,
Some power of quick suggestion how to save,
Touching the living soul as from above.

An influence from the Earth from those dead hearts
So passionate once, so deep, so truly kind,
That in the living child the spirit starts,
Feeling companioned still, not left behind.

Surely above these fields a spirit broods
A sense of many watchers muttering near
Of the lone Downland with the forlorn woods
Loved to the death, inestimably dear.

A muttering from beyond the veils of Death
From long-dead men, to whom this quiet scene
Came among blinding tears with the last breath,
The dying soldier's vision of his queen.

All the unspoken worship of those lives
Spent in forgotten wars at other calls
Glimmers upon these fields where evening drives
Beauty like breath, so gently darkness falls.

Darkness that makes the meadows holier still,
The elm-trees sadden in the hedge, a sigh
Moves in the beech-clump on the haunted hill,
The rising planets deepen in the sky,

And silence broods like spirit on the brae,
A glimmering moon begins, the moonlight runs
Over the grasses of the ancient way
Rutted this morning by the passing guns.

[Extract I from 'Biography']

When I am buried, all my thoughts and acts
Will be reduced to lists of dates and facts,
And long before this wandering flesh is rotten
The dates which made me will be all forgotten;
And none will know the gleam there used to be
About the feast-days freshly kept by me,
But men will call the golden hour of bliss
'About this time,' or 'shortly after this.'

Men do not heed the rungs by which men climb
Those glittering steps, those milestones upon Time,
Those tombstones of dead selves, those hours of birth,
Those moments of the soul in years of earth.
They mark the height achieved, the main result,
The power of freedom in the perished cult,
The power of boredom in the dead man's deeds,
Not the bright moments of the sprinkled seeds.

[Extract II from 'Biography']

Best trust the happy moments. What they gave
Makes man less fearful of the certain grave,
And gives his work compassion and new eyes,
The days that make us happy make us wise.

They Closed Her Eyes

(from the Spanish of Don Gustavo A. Becquér)

They closed her eyes,
They were still open;
They hid her face
With a white linen,
And some sobbing,
Others in silence,
From the sad bedroom
All came away.

The nightlight in a dish
Burned on the floor;
It threw on the wall
The bed's shadow,
And in that shadow
One saw some times
Drawn in sharp line
The body's shape.

The dawn appeared.
At its first whiteness,
With its thousand noises,
The town awoke.
Before that contrast
Of light and darkness,
Of life and strangeness,
I thought a moment.
>   *My God, how lonely*
>   *The dead are.*

On the shoulders of men
To church they bore her,
And in a chapel
They left her bier.
There they surrounded
Her pale body
With yellow candles
And black stuffs.

At the last stroke
Of the ringing for the souls
An old crone finished
Her last prayers.
She crossed the narrow nave,
The doors moaned,
And the holy place
Remained deserted.

From a clock one heard
The measured ticking,
And from a candle
The guttering.
All things there
Were so dark and mournful,
So cold and rigid,
That I thought a moment –
  My God, how lonely
  The dead are!

From the high belfry
The tongue of iron
Clanged, giving out
A last farewell.
Crape on their clothes,
Her friends and kindred
Passed by in line
In homage to her.

In the last vault,
Dark and narrow,
The pickaxe opened
A niche at one end;
They laid her away there.
Soon they bricked the place up,
And with a gesture
Bade grief farewell.

Pickaxe on shoulder,
The gravedigger,
Singing between his teeth
Passed out of sight
The night came down
It was all silent.
Alone in darkness,
I thought a moment –
  My God, how lonely
  The dead are!

In the dark nights
Of bitter winter,
When the wind makes
The rafters creak,
When the violent rain
Lashes the windows,
Lonely I remember
That poor girl.

There falls the rain
With its noise eternal
There the north wind
Fights with the rain.
Stretched in the hollow
Of the damp bricks,
Perhaps her bones
Freeze with the cold.

Does the dust return to dust?
Does the soul fly to heaven?
Or is all vile matter,
Rottenness, filthiness?
I know not, but
There is something – something –
Something which gives me
Loathing, terror,
To leave the dead
So alone, so wretched.

from The Faithful

[Kurano's Song]

Once, very long ago,
When there was still the sun,
Before these times, before
The light was darkened,
One whom we used to know
Made life most noble; one
Who would have changed the world
Had people hearkened.

It was a dream. Perhaps
Time drugs the soul with dreams
To all but blind desire
For high attempt;
Then the intense string snaps;
The project seems
A hearth without a fire,
A madness dreamt.

from Good Friday

['They cut my face...']

They cut my face, there's blood upon my brow.
So, let it run, I am an old man now,
An old, blind beggar picking filth for bread.
Once I wore silk, drank wine,
Spent gold on women, feasted, all was mine;
But this uneasy current in my head
Burst, one full moon, and cleansed me, then I saw
Truth like a perfect crystal, life its flaw,
I told the world, but I was mad, they said.

I had a valley farm above a brook,
My sheep bells there were sweet,
And in the summer heat
My mill wheels turned, yet all these things they took;
Ah, and I gave them, all things I forsook
But that green blade of wheat,
My own soul's courage, that they did not take.

I will go on, although my old heart ache.
Not long, not long.
Soon I shall pass behind
This changing veil to that which does not change,
My tired feet will range
In some green valley of eternal mind
Where Truth is daily like the water's song.

['The wild duck...']

The wild duck, stringing through the sky,
Are south away.
Their green necks glitter as they fly,
The lake is gray.
So still, so lone, the fowler never heeds.
The wind goes rustle, rustle, through the reeds.

*   *   *   *

There they find peace to have their own wild souls.
In that still lake,
Only the moonrise or the wind controls
The way they take,
Through the gray reeds, the cocking moorhen's lair,
Rippling the pool, or over leagues of air.

*   *   *   *

Not thus, not thus are the wild souls of men.
No peace for those
Who step beyond the blindness of the pen
To where the skies unclose.
For them the spitting mob, the cross, the crown of thorns,
The bull gone mad, the saviour on his horns.

* * * *

Beauty and peace have made,
No peace, no still retreat,
No solace, none.
Only the unafraid
Before life's roaring street
Touch Beauty's feet,
Know Truth, do as God bade,
Become God's son.

[*Pause.*]

Darkness, come down, cover a brave man's pain,
Let the bright soul go back to God again.
Cover that tortured flesh, it only serves
To hold that thing which other power nerves.
Darkness, come down, let it be midnight here,
In the dark night the untroubled soul sings clear.

[*It darkens.*]

I have been scourged, blinded and crucified,
My blood burns on the stones of every street
In every town; wherever people meet
I have been hounded down, in anguish died.

[*It darkens.*]

The creaking door of flesh rolls slowly back;
Nerve by red nerve the links of living crack,
Loosing the soul to tread another track.
Beyond the pain, beyond the broken clay,
A glimmering country lies
Where life is being wise,

All of the beauty seen by truthful eyes
Are lilies there, growing beside the way.
Those golden ones will loose the torted hands,
Smooth the scarred brow, gather the breaking soul,
Whose earthly moments drop like falling sands
To leave the spirit whole.
Now darkness is upon the face of the earth.

['Only a penny...']

[*Only the* MADMAN *remains. He takes lilies from a box and begins to tie them in bunches.*]

Only a penny, a penny,
Lilies brighter than any,
Lilies whiter than snow. [*He feels that he is alone.*]
Beautiful lilies grow
Wherever the truth so sweet
Has trodden with bloody feet,
Has stood with a bloody brow.
Friend, it is over now,
The passion, the sweat, the pains,
Only the truth remains. [*He lays lilies down.*]

*   *   *   *

I cannot see what others see;
Wisdom alone is kind to me,
Wisdom that comes from Agony.

*   *   *   *

Wisdom that lives in the pure skies,
The untouched star, the spirit's eyes:
O Beauty, touch me, make me wise.

from Sonnets and Poems (Letchworth: Garden City Press)

V

Here in the self is all that man can know
Of Beauty, all the wonder, all the power,
All the unearthly colour, all the glow,
Here in the self which withers like a flower,
Here in the self which fades as hours pass,
And droops and dies and rots and is forgotten
Sooner, by ages, than the mirroring glass
In which it sees its glory still unrotten.
Here in the flesh, within the flesh, behind,
Swift in the blood and throbbing on the bone,
Beauty herself, the universal mind,
Eternal April wandering alone,
The god, the holy ghost, the atoning lord,
Here in the flesh, the never yet explored.

VI

Flesh, I have knocked at many a dusty door,
Gone down full many a windy midnight lane,
Probed in old walls and felt along the floor,
Pressed in blind hope the lighted window-pane.
But useless all, though sometimes when the moon
Was full in heaven and the sea was full,
Along my body's alleys came a tune
Played in the tavern by the Beautiful.
Then for an instant I have felt at point
To find and seize her, whosoe'er she be,
Whether some saint whose glory doth anoint
Those whom she loves, or but a part of me,
Or something that the things not understood
Make for their uses out of flesh and blood.

87

VII

But all has passed, the tune has died away,
The glamour gone, the glory; is it chance?
Is the unfeeling mud stabbed by a ray
Cast by an unseen splendour's great advance?
Or does the glory gather crumb by crumb
Unseen, within, as coral islands rise
Till suddenly the apparitions come
Above the surface, looking at the skies?
Or does sweet Beauty dwell in lovely things
Scattering the holy hintings of her name
In women, in dear friends, in flowers, in springs,
In the brook's voice, for us to catch the same?
Or is it we who are Beauty, we who ask?
We by whose gleams the world fulfils its task.

VIII

These myriad days, these many thousand hours,
A man's long life, so choked with dusty things,
How little perfect poise with perfect powers,
Joy at the heart and Beauty at the springs.
One hour, or two, or three, in long years scattered,
Sparks from a smithy that have fired a thatch,
Are all that life has given and all that mattered,
The rest, all heaving at a moveless latch.
For these, so many years of useless toil,
Despair, endeavour, and again despair,
Sweat, that the base machine may have its oil,
Idle delight to tempt one everywhere.
A life upon the cross. To make amends,
Three flaming memories that the deathbed ends.

IX

There, on the darkened deathbed, dies the brain
That flared there several times in seventy years.
It cannot lift the silly hand again,
Nor speak, nor sing, it neither sees nor hears.
And muffled mourners put it in the ground
And then go home, and in the earth it lies
Too dark for vision and too deep for sound,
The million cells that made a good man wise.
Yet for a few short years an influence stirs
A sense or wraith or essence of him dead
Which makes insensate things its ministers
To those beloved, his spirit's daily bread,
Then that, too, fades; in book or deed a spark
Lingers, then that, too, fades; then all is dark.

X

So in the empty sky the stars appear,
Are bright in heaven marching through the sky,
Spinning their planets, each one to his year,
Tossing their fiery hair until they die;
Then in the tower afar the watcher sees
The sun, that burned, less noble than it was,
Less noble still, until by dim degrees
No spark of him is specklike in his glass.
Then blind and dark in heaven the sun proceeds,
Vast, dead and hideous, knocking on his moons,
Till crashing on his like creation breeds.
Striking such life, a constellation swoons,
From dead things striking fire a new sun springs
New fire, new life, new planets with new wings.

XI

It may be so with us, that in the dark,
When we have done with Time and wander Space,
Some meeting of the blind may strike a spark,
And to Death's empty mansion give a grace.
It may be, that the loosened soul may find
Some new delight of living without limbs,
Bodiless joy of flesh-untrammelled mind,
Peace like a sky where starlike spirit swims.
It may be, that the million cells of sense,
Loosed from their seventy years' adhesion, pass
Each to some joy of changed experience
Weight in the earth or glory in the grass.
It may be that we cease; we cannot tell.
Even if we cease life is a miracle.

XII

What am I, Life? A thing of watery salt
Held in cohesion by unresting cells
Which work they know not why, which never halt,
Myself unwitting where their master dwells.
I do not bid them, yet they toil, they spin;
A world which uses me as I use them,
Nor do I know which end or which begin,
Nor which to praise, which pamper, which condemn.
So, like a marvel in a marvel set,
I answer to the vast, as wave by wave
The sea of air goes over, dry or wet,
Or the full moon comes swimming from her cave,
Or the great sun comes north, this myriad I
Tingles, not knowing how, yet wondering why.

XIII

If I could get within this changing I,
This ever altering thing, which yet persists,
Keeping the features it is reckoned by,
While each component atom breaks or twists,
If, wandering past strange groups of shifting forms,
Cells, at their hidden marvels hard at work
Pale from much toil, or red from sudden storms,
I might attain to where the Rulers lurk.
If, pressing past the guards in those grey gates,
The brain's most folded, intertwisted shell,
I might attain to that which alters fates,
The King, the supreme self, the Master Cell;
Then, on Man's earthly peak, I might behold
The unearthly self beyond, unguessed, untold.

XIV

What is this atom which contains the whole,
This miracle which needs adjuncts so strange,
This, which imagined God and is the soul,
The steady star persisting amid change?
What waste, that smallness of such power should need
Such clumsy tools so easy to destroy,
Such wasteful servants difficult to feed,
Such indirect dark avenues to joy.
Why, if its business is not mainly earth,
Should it demand such heavy chains to sense?
A heavenly thing demands a swifter birth,
A quicker hand to act intelligence;
An earthly thing were better like the rose,
At peace with clay from which its beauty grows.

XV

Ah, we are neither heaven nor earth, but men;
Something that uses and despises both,
That takes its earth's contentment in the pen,
Then sees the world's injustice and is wroth,
And flinging off youth's happy promise, flies
Up to some breach, despising earthly things,
And, in contempt of hell and heaven, dies
Rather than bear some yoke of priests or kings.
Our joys are not of heaven nor earth, but man's,
A woman's beauty or a child's delight,
The trembling blood when the discoverer scans
The sought-for world, the guessed-at satellite;
The ringing scene, the stone at point to blush
For unborn men to look at and say 'Hush.'

XVI

Roses are beauty, but I never see
Those blood drops from the burning heart of June
Glowing like thought upon the living tree
Without a pity that they die so soon,
Die into petals, like those roses old,
Those women, who were summer in men's hearts
Before the smile upon the Sphinx was cold
Or sand had hid the Syrian and his arts.
O myriad dust of beauty that lies thick
Under our feet that not a single grain
But stirred and moved in beauty and was quick
For one brief moon and died nor lived again;
But when the moon rose lay upon the grass
Pasture to living beauty, life that was.

XVII

Over the church's door they moved a stone,
And there, unguessed, forgotten, mortared up,
Lay the priest's cell where he had lived alone.
There was his ashy hearth, his drinking cup,
There was his window whence he saw the host,
The god whose beauty quickened bread and wine,
The skeleton of a religion lost,
The ghostless bones of what had been divine.
O many a time the dusty masons come
Knocking their trowels in the stony brain
To cells where perished priests had once a home,
Or where devout brows pressed the window pane,
Watching the thing made God, the god whose bones
Bind underground our soul's foundation stones.

XIX

O little self, within whose smallness lies
All that man was, and is, and will become,
Atom unseen that comprehends the skies
And tells the tracks by which the planets roam;
That, without moving, knows the joys of wings,
The tiger's strength, the eagle's secrecy,
And in the hovel can consort with kings,
Or clothe a god with his own mystery.
O with what darkness do we cloak thy light,
What dusty folly gather thee for food,
Thou who alone art knowledge and delight,
The heavenly bread, the beautiful, the good.
O living self, O god, O morning star,
Give us thy light, forgive us what we are.

XX

I went into the fields, but you were there
Waiting for me, so all the summer flowers
Were only glimpses of your starry powers;
Beautiful and inspired dust they were.
I went down by the waters, and a bird
Sang with your voice in all the unknown tones
Of all that self of you I have not heard,
So that my being felt you to the bones.
I went into my house, and shut the door
To be alone, but you were there with me;
All beauty in a little room may be,
Though the roof lean and muddy be the floor.
Then in my bed I bound my tired eyes
To make a darkness for my weary brain;
But like a presence you were there again,
Being and real, beautiful and wise,
So that I could not sleep, and cried aloud,
'You strange grave thing, what is it you would say?'
The redness of your dear lips dimmed to grey,
The waters ebbed, the moon hid in a cloud.

XXVI

Wherever beauty has been quick in clay
Some effluence of it lives, a spirit dwells,
Beauty that death can never take away
Mixed with the air that shakes the flower bells;
So that by waters where the apples fall,
Or in lone glens, or valleys full of flowers,
Or in the streets where bloody tidings call,
The haunting waits the mood that makes it ours.
Then at a turn, a word, an act, a thought,
Such difference comes; the spirit apprehends
That place's glory; for where beauty fought
Under the veil the glory never ends;
But the still grass, the leaves, the trembling flower
Keep, through dead time, that everlasting hour.

XXX

Not for the anguish suffered is the slur,
Not for the women's mocks, the taunts of men;
No, but because you never welcomed her,
Her of whose beauty I am only the pen.
There was a dog, dog-minded, with dog's eyes,
Damned by a dog's brute-nature to be true.
Something within her made his spirit wise;
He licked her hand, he knew her; not so you.
When all adulterate beauty has gone by,
When all inanimate matter has gone down,
We will arise and walk, that dog and I,
The only two who knew her in the town.
We'll range the pleasant mountains side by side,
Seeking the blood-stained flowers where Christs have died.

XXXIII

You will remember me in days to come,
With love, or pride, or pity, or contempt,
So will my friends (not many friends, yet some),
When this my life will be a dream out-dreamt;
And one, remembering friendship by the fire,
And one, remembering love time in the dark,
And one, remembering unfulfilled desire,
Will sigh, perhaps, yet be beside the mark;
For this my body with its wandering ghost
Is nothing solely but an empty grange,
Dark in a night that owls inhabit most,
Yet when the King rides by there comes a change;
The windows gleam, the cresset's fiery hair
Blasts the blown branch and beauty lodges there.

XXXVII

If all be governed by the moving stars,
If passing planets bring events to be,
Searing the face of Time with bloody scars,
Drawing men's souls even as the moon the sea,
If as they pass they make a current pass
Across man's life and heap it to a tide,
We are but pawns, ignobler than the grass
Cropped by the beast and crunched and tossed aside.
Is all this beauty that does inhabit heaven
Trail of a planet's fire? Is all this lust
A chymic means by warring stars contriven
To bring the violets out of Cæsar's dust?
Better be grass, or in some hedge unknown
The spilling rose whose beauty is its own.

XXXVIII

In emptiest furthest heaven where no stars are,
Perhaps some planet of our master sun
Still rolls an unguessed orbit round its star,
Unthought, unseen, unknown of anyone.
Roving dead space according to its law,
Casting our light on burnt-out suns and blind,
Singing in the frozen void its word of awe,
One wandering thought in all that idiot mind.
And, in some span of many a thousand year,
Passing through heaven its influence may arouse
Beauty unguessed in those who habit here,
And men may rise with glory on their brows
And feel new life like fire, and see the old
Fall from them dead, the bronze's broken mould.

XL

For, like an outcast from the city, I
Wander the desert strewn with travellers' bones,
Having no comrade but the starry sky
Where the tuned planets ride their floating thrones.
I pass old ruins where the kings caroused
In cups long shards from vines long since decayed,
I tread the broken brick where queens were housed
In beauty's time ere beauty was betrayed,
And in the ceaseless pitting of the sand
On monolith and pyle, I see the dawn
Making those skeletons of beauty grand
By fire that comes as darkness is withdrawn,
And, in that fire, the art of men to come
Shines with such glow I bless my martyrdom.

XLI

Death lies in wait for you, you wild thing in the wood,
Shy-footed beauty dear, half-seen, half-understood,
Glimpsed in the beech-wood dim and in the dropping fir,
Shy like a fawn and sweet and beauty's minister.
Glimpsed as in flying clouds by night the little moon,
A wonder, a delight, a paleness passing soon.

Only a moment held, only an hour seen,
Only an instant known in all that life has been,
One instant in the sand to drink that gush of grace,
The beauty of your way, the marvel of your face.

Death lies in wait for you, but few short hours he gives;
I perish even as you by whom all spirit lives.
Come to me, spirit, come, and fill my hour of breath
With hours of life in life that pay no toll to death.

XLII

They called that broken hedge The Haunted Gate.
Strange fires (they said) burnt there at moonless times.
Evil was there, men never went there late,
The darkness there was quick with threatened crimes.
And then one digging in that bloodied clay
Found, but a foot below, a rotted chest.
Coins of the Romans, tray on rusted tray,
Hurriedly heaped there by a digger prest.
So that one knew how, centuries before,
Some Roman flying from the sack by night,
Digging in terror there to hide his store,
Sweating his pick, by windy lantern light,
Had stamped his anguish on that place's soul,
So that it knew and could rehearse the whole.

XLIV

Go, spend your penny, Beauty, when you will,
In the grave's darkness let the stamp be lost.
The water still will bubble from the hill,
And April quick the meadows with her ghost;
Over the grass the daffodils will shiver,
The primroses with their pale beauty abound,
The blackbird be a lover and make quiver
With his glad singing the great soul of the ground;
So that if the body rot, it will not matter;
Up in the earth the great game will go on,
The coming of spring and the running of the water,
And the young things glad of the womb's darkness gone.
And the joy we felt will be a part of the glory
In the lover's kiss that makes the old couple's story.

XLVII

Let that which is to come be as it may,
Darkness, extinction, justice, life intense,
The flies are happy in the summer day,
Flies will be happy many summers hence.
Time with his antique breeds that built the Sphinx,
Time with her men to come whose wings will tower,
Poured and will pour, not as the wise man thinks,
But with blind force, to each his little hour.
And when the hour has struck, comes death or change,
Which, whether good or ill we cannot tell,
But the blind planet will wander through her range
Bearing men like us who will serve as well.
The sun will rise, the winds that ever move
Will blow our dust that once were men in love.

from Sonnets and Poems (Lollingdon: John Masefield)

XXXIV

If Beauty be at all, if, beyond sense,
There be a wisdom piercing into brains,
Why should the glory wait on impotence,
Biding its time till blood is in the veins?

There is no beauty, but, when thought is quick,
Out of the noisy sickroom of ourselves
Some flattery comes to try to cheat the sick,
Some drowsy drug is groped for on the shelves.

There is no beauty, for we tread a scene
Red to the eye with blood of living things;
Thought is but joy from murder that has been,
Life is but brute at war upon its kings.

There is no beauty, nor could beauty care
For us, this dust, that men make everywhere.

XXXV

O wretched man, that, for a little mile,
Crawls beneath heaven for his brother's blood,
Whose days the planets number with their style,
To whom all earth is slave, all living, food;

O withering man, within whose folded shell,
Lies yet the seed, the spirit's quickening corn,
That Time and Sun will change out of the cell
Into green meadows, in the world unborn;

If Beauty be a dream, do but resolve
And fire shall come, that in the stubborn clay
Works to make perfect till the rocks dissolve,
The barriers burst and beauty takes her way,

Beauty herself, within whose blossoming Spring
Even wretched man shall clap his hands and sing.

XXXVI

Night is on the downland, on the lonely moorland,
On the hills where the wind goes over sheep-bitten turf,
Where the bent grass beats upon the unploughed poorland
And the pine woods roar like the surf.

Here the Roman lived on the wind-barren lonely,
Dark now and haunted by the moorland fowl;
None comes here now but the peewit only,
And moth-like death in the owl.

Beauty was here, on this beetle-droning downland;
The thought of a Cæsar in the purple came
From his palace by the Tiber in the Roman townland
To this wind-swept hill with no name.

Lonely Beauty came here and was here in sadness,
Brave as a thought on the frontier of the mind,
In the camp of the wild upon the march of madness,
The bright-eyed Queen of the blind.

Now where Beauty was are the wind-withered gorses
Moaning like old men in the hill-wind's blast,
The flying sky is dark with running horses
And the night is full of the past.

from Gallipoli

Epilogue

Even so was wisdom proven blind,
So courage failed, so strength was chained;
Even so the gods, whose seeing mind
Is not as ours, ordained.

from Salt-Water Poems and Ballads

The New Bedford Whaler

There was a 'Bedford Whaler put out to hunt for oil,
With a try-works in amidships where chunks of whale could boil,
And a fo'c's'le, wet and frowsy, where whalers' crews could gam,
And her captain came from 'Bedford and did not give a cent,
So over the bar from 'Bedford to hunt the whale she went.

But never a whale she sighted for eight and forty moons,
She never lowered her boats in chase nor reddened her harpoons,
So home she went to 'Bedford, where her owners came to ask,
'How many tons of whalebone, cap, and how much oil in cask?'

The captain turned his tobacco inside his weather cheek,
And he said 'At least the Bible says, blessed are they who seek.
We've been at sea four years and more and never seen a whale,
We haven't a lick of oil on board but we've had a darned good sail.'

from Lollingdon Downs and other poems, with sonnets

III

Out of the special cell's most special sense
Came the suggestion when the light was sweet;
All skill, all beauty, all magnificence,
Are hints so caught, man's glimpse of the complete.
And, though the body rots, that sense survives;
Being of life's own essence, it endures
(Fruit of the spirit's tillage in men's lives)
Round all this ghost that wandering flesh immures.
That is our friend, who, when the iron brain
Assails, or the earth clogs, or the sun hides,
Is the good God to whom none calls in vain,
Man's Achieved Good, which, being Life, abides:
The man-made God, that man in happy breath
Makes in despite of Time and dusty Death.

V

I could not sleep for thinking of the sky,
The unending sky, with all its million suns
Which turn their planets everlastingly
In nothing, where the fire-haired comet runs.
If I could sail that nothing, I should cross
Silence and emptiness with dark stars passing;
Then, in the darkness, see a point of gloss
Burn to a glow, and glare, and keep amassing,
And rage into a sun with wandering planets,
And drop behind; and then, as I proceed,
See his last light upon his last moon's granites
Die to a dark that would be night indeed:
Night where my soul might sail a million years
In nothing, not even Death, not even tears.

VI

How did the nothing come, how did these fires,
These million-leagues of fires, first toss their hair,
Licking the moons from heaven in their ires,
Flinging them forth for them to wander there?
What was the Mind? Was it a mind which thought?
Or chance? or law? or conscious law? or power?
Or a vast balance by vast clashes wrought?
Or Time at trial with Matter for an hour?
Or is it all a body where the cells
Are living things supporting something strange,
Whose mighty heart the singing planet swells
As it shoulders nothing in unending change?
Is this green earth of many-peopled pain
Part of a life, a cell within a brain?

VII

It may be so; but let the unknown be.
We, on this earth, are servants of the sun:
Out of the sun comes all the quick in me,
His golden touch is life to everyone.
His power it is that makes us spin through space;
His youth is April and his manhood bread;
Beauty is but a looking on his face;
He clears the mind, he makes the roses red.
What he may be, who knows? But we are his;
We roll through nothing round him, year by year,
The withering leaves upon a tree which is,
Each with his greed, his little power, his fear,
What we may be, who knows? But every one
Is dust on dust a servant of the sun.

IX

What is this life which uses living cells
It knows not how nor why, for no known end,
This soul of man upon whose fragile shells
Of blood and brain his very powers depend?
Pour out its little blood or touch its brain,
The thing is helpless, gone, no longer known;
The carrion cells are never man again,
No hand relights the little candle blown.
It comes not from Without, but from the sperm
Fed in the womb; it is a man-made thing
That takes from man its power to live a term,
Served by live cells of which it is the King.
Can it be blood and brain? It is most great.
Through blood and brain alone it wrestles Fate.

X

Can it be blood and brain, this transient force
Which, by an impulse, seizes flesh and grows
To man, the thing less splendid than the horse,
More blind than owls, less lovely than the rose?
O, by a power unknown it works the cells
Of blood and brain; it has the power to see
Beyond the apparent thing the something else
Which it inspires dust to bring to be.
Both blood and brain are its imperfect tools,
Easily wrecked, soon worn, slow to attain;
Only by years of toil the master rules
To lovely ends those servants, blood and brain.
And Death, a touch, a germ, has still the force
To make him ev'n as the rose, the owl, the horse.

XI

Not only blood and brain its servants are;
There is a finer power that needs no slaves,
Whose lovely service distance cannot bar,
Nor the green sea with all her hell of waves;
Nor snowy mountains, nor the desert sand,
Nor heat, nor storm, it bends to no control;
It is a stretching of the spirit's hand
To touch the brother's or the sister's soul;
So that from darkness in the narrow room
I can step forth and be about her heart,
Needing no star, no lantern in the gloom,
No word from her, no pointing on the chart,
Only red knowledge of a window flung
Wide to the night, and calling without tongue.

XXIV

Here the legion halted, here the ranks were broken,
And the men fell out to gather wood;
And the green wood smoked, and bitter words were spoken,
And the trumpets called to food.

And the sentry on the rampart saw the distance dying
In the smoke of distance blue and far,
And heard the curlew calling and the owl replying
As the night came cold with one star;

And thought of home beyond, over moorland, over marshes,
Over hills, over the sea, across the plains, across the pass,
By a bright sea trodden by the ships of Tarshis,
The farm, with cicadæ in the grass.

And thought, as I: 'Perhaps, I may be done with living
To-morrow, when we fight. I shall see those souls no more.
O beloved souls, be beloved in forgiving
The deeds and the words that make me sore.'

from Reynard the Fox

['The fox was strong…']

The fox was strong, he was full of running,
He could run for an hour and then be cunning,
But the cry behind him made him chill,
They were nearer now and they meant to kill.
They meant to run him until his blood
Clogged on his heart as his brush with mud,
Till his back bent up and his tongue hung flagging,
And his belly and brush were filthed from dragging.
Till he crouched stone-still, dead-beat and dirty,
With nothing but teeth against the thirty.
And all the way to that blinding end
He would meet with men and have none his friend:
Men to holloa and men to run him,
With stones to stagger and yells to stun him;
Men to head him, with whips to beat him,
Teeth to mangle and mouths to eat him.
And all the way, that wild high crying,
To cold his blood with the thought of dying,
The horn and the cheer, and the drum-like thunder
Of the horsehooves stamping the meadows under.
He upped his brush and went with a will
For the Sarsen Stones on Wan Dyke Hill.

['And here, as he ran to the huntsman's yelling...']

And here, as he ran to the huntsman's yelling,
The fox first felt that the pace was telling;
His body and lungs seemed all grown old,
His legs less certain, his heart less bold,
The hound-noise nearer, the hill-slope steeper,
The thud in the blood of his body deeper.
His pride in his speed, his joy in the race
Were withered away, for what use was pace?
He had run his best, and the hounds ran better.
Then the going worsened, the earth was wetter.
Then his brush drooped down till it sometimes dragged,
And his fur felt sick and his chest was tagged
With taggles of mud, and his pads seemed lead;
It was well for him he'd an earth ahead.
Down he went to the brook and over,
Out of the corn and into the clover,
Over the slope that the Wan Brook drains,
Past Battle Tump where they earthed the Danes,
Then up the hill that the Wan Dyke rings
Where the Sarsen Stones stand grand like kings.

The End of the Run

For a minute he ran and heard no sound,
Then a whimper came from a questing hound,
Then a 'This way, beauties,' and then 'Leu, Leu,'
The floating laugh of the horn that blew.
Then the cry again, and the crash and rattle
Of the shrubs burst back as they ran to battle,
Till the wood behind seemed risen from root,
Crying and crashing, to give pursuit,
Till the trees seemed hounds and the air seemed cry,
And the earth so far that he needs but die,
Die where he reeled in the woodland dim,
With a hound's white grips in the spine of him;
For one more burst he could spurt, and then
Wait for the teeth, and the wrench, and men.

* * * *

He made his spurt for the Mourne End rocks.
The air blew rank with the taint of fox;
The yews gave way to a greener space
Of great stones strewn in a grassy place.
And there was his earth at the great grey shoulder,
Sunk in the ground, of a granite boulder.
A dry, deep burrow with rocky roof,
Proof against crowbars, terrier-proof,
Life to the dying, rest for bones.

* * * *

The earth was stopped; it was filled with stones.

* * * *

Then, for a moment, his courage failed,
His eyes looked up as his body quailed,
Then the coming of death, which all things dread,
Made him run for the wood ahead.

109

* * * *

The taint of fox was rank on the air,
He knew, as he ran, there were foxes there.
His strength was broken, his heart was bursting,
His bones were rotten, his throat was thirsting;
His feet were reeling, his brush was thick
From dragging the mud, and his brain was sick.

* * * *

He thought as he ran of his old delight
In the wood in the moon in an April night,
His happy hunting, his winter loving,
The smells of things in the midnight roving,
The look of his dainty-nosing, red,
Clean-felled dam with her footpad's tread;
Of his sire, so swift, so game, so cunning,
With craft in his brain and power of running;
Their fights of old when his teeth drew blood,
Now he was sick, with his coat all mud.

* * * *

He crossed the covert, he crawled the bank,
To a meuse in the thorns, and there he sank,
With his ears flexed back and his teeth shown white,
In a rat's resolve for a dying bite.

* * * *

And there, as he lay, he saw the vale,
That a struggling sunlight silvered pale:
The Deerlip Brook like a strip of steel,
The Nun's Wood Yews where the rabbits squeal,
The great grass square of the Roman Fort,
And the smoke in the elms at Crendon Court.

* * * *

And above the smoke in the elm-tree tops
Was the beech-clump's blur, Blown Hilcote Copse,
Where he and his mates had long made merry
In the bloody joys of the rabbit-herry.

* * * *

And there as he lay and looked, the cry
Of the hounds at head came rousing by;
He bent his bones in the blackthorn dim.

* * * *

But the cry of the hounds was not for him.
Over the fence with a crash they went,
Belly to grass, with a burning scent;
Then came Dansey, yelling to Bob:
'They've changed! Oh, damn it! now here's a job.'
And Bob yelled back: 'Well, we cannot turn 'em,
It's Jumper and Antic, Tom, we'll learn 'em!
We must just go on, and I hope we kill.'
They followed hounds down the Mourne End Hill.

* * * *

The fox lay still in the rabbit-meuse,
On the dry brown dust of the plumes of yews.
In the bottom below a brook went by,
Blue, in a patch, like a streak of sky.
There one by one, with a clink of stone,
Came a red or dark coat on a horse half-blown.
And man to man with a gasp for breath
Said: 'Lord, what a run! I'm fagged to death.'

* * * *

After an hour no riders came,
The day drew by like an ending game;
A robin sang from a pufft red breast,
The fox lay quiet and took his rest.
A wren on a tree-stump carolled clear,

Then the starlings wheeled in a sudden sheer,
The rooks came home to the twiggy hive
In the elm-tree tops which the winds do drive.
Then the noise of the rooks fell slowly still,
And the lights came out in the Clench Brook Mill;
Then a pheasant cocked, then an owl began,
With the cry that curdles the blood of man.

* * * *

The stars grew bright as the yews grew black;
The fox rose stiffly and stretched his back.
He flaired the air, then he padded out
To the valley below him, dark as doubt,
Winter-thin with the young green crops,
For old Cold Crendon and Hilcote Copse.

* * * *

As he crossed the meadows at Naunton Larking
The dogs in the town all started barking,
For with feet all bloody and flanks all foam,
The hounds and the hunt were limping home;
Limping home in the dark dead-beaten,
The hounds all rank from a fox they'd eaten.
Dansey saying to Robin Dawe:
'The fastest and longest I ever saw.'
And Robin answered: 'Oh, Tom, 'twas good!
I thought they'd changed in the Mourne End Wood,
But now I feel that they did not change.
We've had a run that was great and strange;
And to kill in the end, at dusk, on grass!
We'll turn to the Cock and take a glass,
For the hounds, poor souls! are past their forces;
And a gallon of ale for our poor horses,
And some bits of bread for the hounds, poor things!
After all they've done (for they've done like kings),
Would keep them going till we get in.
We had it alone from Nun's Wood Whin.'

Then Tom replied: 'If they changed or not,
There've been few runs longer and none more hot;
We shall talk of to-day until we die.'

* * * *

The stars grew bright in the winter sky,
The wind came keen with a tang of frost,
The brook was troubled for new things lost,
The copse was happy for old things found,
The fox came home and he went to ground.

* * * *

And the hunt came home and the hounds were fed,
They climbed to their bench and went to bed;
The horses in stable loved their straw.
'Good-night, my beauties,' said Robin Dawe.

* * * *

Then the moon came quiet and flooded full
Light and beauty on clouds like wool,
On a feasted fox at rest from hunting,
In the beech-wood grey where the brocks were grunting.

* * * *

The beech-wood grey rose dim in the night
With moonlight fallen in pools of light,
The long dead leaves on the ground were rimed;
A clock struck twelve and the church-bells chimed.

from Enslaved and other poems

[Gerard's Answer]

He rose up in his place and rent his dress.
'Let them be ganched upon the hooks,' he cried,
'Throughout to-day, but not till they have died.
Then gather all the slaves, and flay these three
Alive, before them, that the slaves may see
What comes to dogs who try to get away.
So, ganch the three.'

*　*　*　*

　　　　Then Gerard answered: 'Stay.
Before you fling us to the hooks, hear this.
There are two laws, and men may go amiss
Either by breaking or by keeping one.
There is man's law by which man's work is done.
Your galleys rowed, your palace kept in state,
Your victims ganched or headed on the gate,
And accident has bent us to its yoke.

*　*　*　*

We break it: death; but it is better broke.

*　*　*　*

You know, you Khalif, by what death you reign,
What force of fraud, what cruelty of pain,
What spies and prostitutes support your power,
And help your law to run its little hour:
We, who are but ourselves, defy it all.

*　*　*　*

'We were free people till you made us thrall.
I was a sailor whom you took at sea

While sailing home. This woman that you see
You broke upon with murder in the night,
To drag her here to die for your delight.
This young man is her lover.
                               When he knew
That she was taken by your pirate crew,
He followed her to save her, or at least
Be near her in her grief. Man is a beast,
And women are his pasture by your law.
This young man was in safety, and he saw
His darling taken to the slave-girls' pen
Of weeping in the night and beasts of men.
He gave up everything, risked everything,
Came to your galley, took the iron ring,
Rowed at the bitter oar-loom as a slave,
Only for love of her, for hope to save
Her from one bruise of all the many bruises
That fall upon a woman when she loses
Those whom your gang of bloodhounds made her lose.

* * * *

Knowing another law, we could not choose
But stamp your law beneath our feet as dust,
Its bloodshed and its rapine and its lust,
For one clean hour of struggle to be free;
She for her passionate pride of chastity,
He for his love of her, and I because
I'm not too old to glory in the cause
Of generous souls who have harsh measure meted.

* * * *

We did the generous thing and are defeated.
Boast, then, to-night, when you have drunken deep,
Between the singing woman's song and sleep,
That you have tortured to the death three slaves
Who spat upon your law and found their graves
Helping each other in the generous thing.
No mighty triumph for a boast, O King.'

Sonnets

Like bones the ruins of the cities stand,
Like skeletons and skulls with ribs and eyes
Strewn in the saltness of the desert sand
Carved with the unread record of Kings' lies.
Once they were strong with soldiers, loud with voices,
The markets clattered as the carts drove through,
Where now the jackal in the moon rejoices
And the still asp draws death along the dew.
There at the gates the market men paid toll
In bronze and silver pennies, long worn thin;
Wine was a silver penny for a bowl;
Women they had there, and the moon, and sin.
And looking from his tower, the watchman saw
Green fields for miles, the roads, the great King's law.

Now they are gone with all their songs and sins,
Women and men, to dust; their copper penny,
Of living, spent, among these dusty inns;
The glittering One made level with the many.
Their speech is gone, none speaks it, none can read
The pictured writing of their conqueror's march;
The dropping plaster of a faded screed
Ceils with its mildews the decaying arch.
The fields are sand, the streets are fallen stones;
Nothing is bought or sold there, nothing spoken:
The sand hides all, the wind that blows it moans,
Blowing more sand until the plinth is broken.
Day in, day out, no other utterance falls;
Only the sand, pit-pitting on the walls.

None knows what overthrew that city's pride.
Some say, the spotted pestilence arose
And smote them to the marrow, that they died
Till every pulse was dusty; no man knows.
Some say, that foreign Kings with all their hosts
Sieged it with mine and tower till it fell,
So that the sword shred shrieking flesh from ghosts
Till every street was empty; who can tell?
Some think, that in the fields, or in the pit,
Out of the light, in filth, among the rotten,
Insects like sands in number, swift as wit,
Famined the city dead; it is forgotten.
Only the city's bones stand, gaunt in air,
Pocked by the pitting sandspecks everywhere.

So shall we be; so will our cities lie,
Unknown beneath the grasses of the summer,
Walls without roofs, naves open to the sky,
Doors open to the wind, the only comer.
And men will grub the ruins, eyes will peer,
Fingers will grope for pennies, brains will tire
To chronicle the skills we practised here,
While still we breathed the wind and trod the mire.
Oh, like the ghost at dawn, scared by the cock,
Let us make haste, to let the spirit dive
Deep in self's sea, until the deeps unlock
The depths and sunken gold of being alive,
Till, though our Many pass, a Something stands
Aloft through Time that covers all with sands.

The Lemmings

Once in a hundred years the Lemmings come
Westward, in search of food, over the snow;
Westward, until the salt sea drowns them dumb;
Westward, till all are drowned, those Lemmings go.

Once, it is thought, there was a westward land
(Now drowned) where there was food for those starved things,
And memory of the place has burnt its brand
In the little brains of all the Lemming kings.

Perhaps, long since, there was a land beyond
Westward from death, some city, some calm place
Where one could taste God's quiet and be fond
With the little beauty of a human face;

But now the land is drowned. Yet still we press
Westward, in search, to death, to nothingness.

On Growing Old

Be with me, Beauty, for the fire is dying;
My dog and I are old, too old for roving.
Man, whose young passion sets the spindrift flying,
Is soon too lame to march, too cold for loving.
I take the book and gather to the fire,
Turning old yellow leaves; minute by minute
The clock ticks to my heart. A withered wire,
Moves a thin ghost of music in the spinet.
I cannot sail your seas, I cannot wander
Your cornland, nor your hill-land, nor your valleys
Ever again, nor share the battle yonder
Where the young knight the broken squadron rallies.
Only stay quiet while my mind remembers
The beauty of fire from the beauty of embers.

Beauty, have pity! for the strong have power,
The rich their wealth, the beautiful their grace,
Summer of man its sunlight and its flower,
Spring-time of man all April in a face.
Only, as in the jostling in the Strand,
Where the mob thrust or loiters or is loud,
The beggar with the saucer in his hand
Asks only a penny from the passing crowd,
So, from this glittering world with all its fashion,
Its fire, and play of men, its stir, its march,
Let me have wisdom, Beauty, wisdom and passion,
Bread to the soul, rain where the summers parch.
Give me but these, and, though the darkness close,
Even the night will blossom as the rose.

from Right Royal

[*'As a whirl of notes…'*]

As a whirl of notes running in a fugue that men play,
And the thundering follows as the pipe flits away,
And the laughter comes after and the hautboys begin,
So they ran at the hurdle and scattered the whin.
As they leaped to the race-course the sun burst from cloud,
And like tumult in dream came the roar of the crowd.

For to right and to left, now, were crowded men yelling,
And a great cry boomed backward like muffled bells knelling,
And a surge of men running seemed to follow the race,
The horses all trembled and quickened their pace.

As the porpoise, grown weary of his rush through the dim
Of the unlitten silence where the swiftnesses swim,
Learns at sudden the tumult of a clipper bound home
And exults with this playmate and leaps in her foam,

Or as nightingales coming into England in May,
Coming songless at sunset, being worn with the way,
Settle spent in the twilight, drooping head under wing,
Yet are glad when the dark comes, while at moonrise they sing;

Or as fire on a hillside, by happy boys kindled,
That has burnt black a heath-tuft, scorcht a bramble, and dwindled,
Blown by wind yet arises in a wave of flogged flame,
So the souls of those horses to the testing time came.

from King Cole

King Cole Speaks

I have seen sorrow close and suffering close.
I know their ways with men, if any knows.
I know the harshness of the way they have
To loose the base and prison up the brave.
I know that some have found the depth they trod
In deepest sorrow is the heart of God.
Up on the bitter iron there is peace.

In the dark night of prison comes release,
In the black midnight still the cock will crow.
There is a help that the abandoned know
Deep in the heart, that conquerors cannot feel.
Abide in hope the turning of the wheel,
The luck will alter and the star will rise.

Miscellaneous Verse, 1911–1921

Die We Must

Die we must and go to dust,
But let us all be merry;
Let us drink the cocktail down
And let us eat the cherry.

Though we win across the sea,
Let us not be tired;
Yon's the blue and hazy line
Of the lands desired.

Fill the jolly bowl again,
And to hell with sorrow;
We may be the lucky men
At the cards to-morrow.

Darkness brings another day,
So let us sing a chorus;
Though we reach the edge of earth,
There's the sea before us.

White are all the cities there,
All the streets are golden;
All the bonny maids are fair,
Only unbeholden.

Aft the sheet and let her ride
From Vallipo to Trond-em;
Seas are salt and seas are wide,
But the land's beyond them.

Blue and slapping run the waves,
Ebbing out or flowing;
Let us go to life or graves,
Let's at least be going.

[*A Broadside*, No. 12, Fourth Year (Dundrum, Co. Dublin: Cuala Press, May 1912), p. 1]

The Gara River

Oh give me back my ships again
Lonesome Gara, babbling Gara,
My gilded galleons of Spain
Your blue waves sunk oh bonny Gara.
Give me again the *Monte* bold
The beaks that dipped the beams that rolled
The green hulled holy ships of old
That you have foundered babbling Gara.

Give me my youth to have again
Lonesome Gara, hurried Gara,
Link upon link, a golden chain
That Time has plundered, merry Gara.
The green sweet combes, the setting sun,
The fires we lit, the yarns we spun,
The stately ships launched one by one
And one by one, lost, sunny Gara.

[*A Broadside*, No. 3, Sixth Year (Dundrum, Co. Dublin: Cuala Press, August 1913), p. 2]

Skyros

I saw her like a shadow on the sky
In the last light, a blur upon the sea,
Then the gale's darkness put the shadow by
But from one grave that island talked to me;
And, in the midnight, in the breaking storm,
I saw its blackness, a blinking light
And thought: 'So death obscures your gentle form,
So memory strives to make the darkness bright:
And, in that heap of rocks your body lies,
Part of the island till the planet ends,
My gentle comrade, beautiful and wise
Part of this crag this bitter surge offends,
While I, who pass, a little obscure thing
War with this force, and breathe, and am its King.'

[from letter to Edward Marsh, 16 October [1915]. Berg Collection,
New York Public Library]

from King Cole and other poems

The Rider at the Gate

A windy night was blowing on Rome,
The cressets guttered on Cæsar's home,
The fish-boats, moored at the bridge, were breaking
The rush of the river to yellow foam.

The hinges whined to the shutters shaking,
When clip-clop-clep came a horse-hoof raking
The stones of the road at Cæsar's gate;
The spear-butts jarred at the guard's awaking.

'Who goes there?' said the guard at the gate.
'What is the news, that you ride so late?'
'News most pressing, that must be spoken
To Cæsar alone, and that cannot wait.'

'The Cæsar sleeps; you must show a token
That the news suffice that he be awoken.
What is the news, and whence do you come?
For no light cause may his sleep be broken.'

'Out of the dark of the sands I come,
From the dark of death, with news for Rome.
A word so fell that it must be uttered
Though it strike the soul of the Cæsar dumb.'

Cæsar turned in his bed and muttered,
With a struggle for breath the lamp-flame guttered;
Calpurnia heard her husband moan:
                'The house is falling,
The beaten men come into their own.'

'Speak your word,' said the guard at the gate;
'Yes, but bear it to Cæsar straight,
Say "Your murderer's knives are honing,
Your killer's gang is lying in wait."

Out of the wind that is blowing and moaning,
Through the city palace and the country loaning,
I cry, "For the world's sake, Cæsar, beware,
And take this warning as my atoning.

Beware of the Court, of the palace stair,
Of the downcast friend who speaks so fair,
Keep from the Senate, for Death is going
On many men's feet to meet you there."

I, who am dead, have ways of knowing
Of the crop of death that the quick are sowing.
I, who was Pompey, cry it aloud
From the dark of death, from the wind blowing.

I, who was Pompey, once was proud,
Now I lie in the sand without a shroud;
I cry to Cæsar out of my pain,
"Cæsar, beware, your death is vowed."'

The light grew grey on the window-pane,
The windcocks swung in a burst of rain,
The window of Cæsar flung unshuttered,
The horse-hoofs died into wind again.

Cæsar turned in his bed and muttered,
With a struggle for breath the lamp-flame guttered;
Calpurnia heard her husband moan:
                    'The house is falling,
The beaten men come into their own.'

The Haunted

Here, in this darkened room of this old house,
I sit beside the fire. I hear again
Within, the scutter where the mice carouse,
Without, the gutter dropping with the rain.

Opposite, are black shelves of wormy books,
To left, glazed cases, dusty with the same,
Behind, a wall, with rusty guns on hooks,
To right, the fire, that chokes one panting flame.

Over the mantel, black as funeral cloth,
A portrait hangs, a man, whose flesh the worm
Has mawed this hundred years, whose clothes the moth
A century since has channelled to a term.

I cannot see his face: I only know
He stares at me, that man of long ago.

*   *   *   *

I light the candles in the long brass sticks,
I see him now, a pale-eyed, simpering man,
Framed in carved wood, wherein the death-watch ticks,
A most dead face: yet when the work began

That face, the pale puce coat, the simpering smile,
The hands that hold a book, the eyes that gaze,
Moved to the touch of mind a little while.
The painter sat in judgment on his ways:

The painter turned him to and from the light,
Talked about art, or bade him lift his head,
Judged the lips' paleness and the temples' white.
And now his work abides; the man is dead.

But is he dead? This dusty study drear
Creeks in its panels that the man is here.

* * * *

Here, beyond doubt, he lived, in that old day.
'He was a Doctor here,' the student thought.
Here, when the puce was new, that now is grey,
That simpering man his daily practice wrought.

Here he let blood, prescribed the pill and drop,
The leech, the diet; here his verdict given
Brought agonies of hoping to a stop,
Here his condemned confessioners were shriven.

What is that book he holds, the key, too dim
To read, to know? Some little book he wrote,
Forgotten now, but still the key to him.
He sacrificed his vision for his coat.

I see the man; a simpering mask that hid
A seeing mind that simpering men forbid.

* * * *

Those are his books no doubt, untoucht, undusted,
Unread, since last he left them on the shelves,
Octavo sermons that the fox has rusted,
Sides splitting off from brown decaying twelves.

This was his room, this darkness of old death,
This coffin-room with lights like embrasures,
The place is poisonous with him; like a breath
On glass, he stains the spirit; he endures.

Here is his name within the sermon book,
And verse, 'When hungry Worms my Body eat';
He leans across my shoulder as I look,
He who is God or pasture to the wheat.

He who is Dead is still upon the soul
A check, an inhibition, a control.

* * * *

I draw the bolts. I am alone within.
The moonlight through the coloured glass comes faint,
Mottling the passage wall like human skin,
Pale with the breathings left of withered paint.

But others walk the empty house with me,
There is no loneliness within these walls
No more than there is stillness in the sea
Or silence in the eternal waterfalls.

There in the room, to right, they sit at feast;
The dropping grey-beard with the cold blue eye,
The lad, his son, that should have been a priest,
And he, the rake, who made his mother die.

And he, the gambling man, who staked the throw,
They look me through, they follow when I go.

*   *   *   *

They follow with still footing down the hall,
I know their souls, those fellow-tenants mine,
Their shadows dim those colours on the wall,
They point my every gesture with a sign.

That grey-beard cast his aged servant forth
After his forty years of service done,
The gambler supped up riches as the north
Sups with his death the glories of the sun.

The lad betrayed his trust; the rake was he
Who broke two women's hearts to ease his own:
They nudge each other as they look at me,
Shadows, all four, and yet as hard as stone.

And there, he comes, that simpering man, who sold
His mind for coat of puce and penny gold.

*   *   *   *

O ruinous house, within whose corridors
None but the wicked and the mad go free.
(On the dark stairs they wait, behind the doors
They crouch, they watch, or creep to follow me.)

Deep in old blood your ominous bricks are red,
Firm in old bones your walls' foundations stand,
With dead men's passions built upon the dead,
With broken hearts for lime and oaths for sand.

Terrible house, whose horror I have built,
Sin after sin, unseen, as sand that slips
Telling the time, till now the heapèd guilt
Cries, and the planets circle to eclipse.

You only are the Daunter, you alone
Clutch, till I feel your ivy on the bone.

from Odtaa

The Meditation of Highworth Ridden

I have seen flowers come in stony places;
And kindness done by men with ugly faces;
And the gold cup won by the worst horse at the races;
       So I trust, too.

from The Midnight Folk

[Not a Nice Song by Rollicum Bitem]

I crept out of covert and what did I see?
Ow-ow-ow-diddle-ow!
But seven fat bunnies, each waiting for me.
With a poacher's noosey, catch the fat goosey, Ho says Rollicum Bitem.

'O pretty bunnies, let's come for a stroll.'
'O no, no, no; you're a fox.'
'A fox pretty dears; can't you see I'm a mole?'
With a weaselly, stoaty, snap at his throaty, Ho says Rollicum Bitem.

'Let's dance, one by one, arm-in-arm, as dear friends.'
'O certainly, sir, if you please.'
So seven fat bunnies had seven sweet ends…
Hay for a hennerel, snug in my dennerel, Ho says Rollicum Bitem.

[Miss Piney Tricker]

Miss Piney Tricker is a girl whose wisdom is most weighty,
She never went to bed till three till she was over eighty.
When claret red is in her head, she carols from her throttle,
Hurray, hurray, my jolly lads, let's have another bottle!
Tooral-loo.

At ninety-five her chief delight was going out to dances,
At ninety-nine she dazzled men by fire from her glances;
And now that she's a hundred odd, she fills her glass with liquor
And says hurray, my jolly lads, hurrah for Piney Tricker!
Tooral-loo.

[The Wind]

A very queer thing is the wind
I don't know how it beginn'd
And nobody knows where it goes,
It is wind, it beginn'd, and it blows.

[Naggy]

Of all the foods as good as tart,
There's none like pretty Naggy;
He warms the cockles of my heart,
Though he is so cold and baggy.

What though the wise eat mutton pies,
Or pasties made of staggy,
To all the wise I makes replies,
Give me my pretty Naggy.

O let my jaw lay down and gnaw
Until my teeth are jaggy,
Both cooked and raw the Scots whae ha
My ain braw sonsie Naggy.

from The Coming of Christ

[Song of the Chorus]

Man was dark, yet he made himself light; he was weak, yet he daunted
The bull with his herd; he was frail, yet he bitted the horse;
He was mean, yet he went with his flint where the elephant haunted
And made him his house from the rocks and his fence of the gorse.

He got him his bread from the grass and his cup from the clay,
His coat from the beast or the flax or the bird in the tree;
Being finless, he followed the fish to the depth of the bay,
Being wingless, he wove him a sail and adventured to sea.

With his comrades he builded the city and gilded the spires;
His thought proves the age of the rocks and the laws of the sky.
He smithies the ores into beauty and use at his fires,
He has harnessed the air and the waters to do his desires;
His wisdom foretells where the comet or planet come by.

Yet forever his restlessness yearns for a peace upon earth,
For a friend who will speak to his soul from a wisdom more true,
From a city more lasting, than his, in a Kingdom more worth;
His want is a check on his mirth,
And he dies, crying out in his need, and his son cries anew.

The Begetting of Arthur

Uther, the Prince, succeeding to the post
Of Red Pendragon, or Anointed Chief
Of all the Kings in Britain, saw with grief
How jealousy and spite
King against King, let in the heathen host,
Who, coming in their hundreds, found a land
Of warring Kingdoms owning no command,
And therefore sackt, uncheckt, from Tyne to Wight.

So when he took the purple he began,
Among his friends, to build a league of Kings:
Iddoc of Kent, among the Easterlings;
The Orkney pirate, Lot;
Then, from the North, the golden hero, Ban;
And having these, he greatly longed to win
Old Merchyon, King of Cornwall rich in tin,
Whose strength would bind the leaguers like a knot.

None loved King Merchyon: Prince Uther knew
That he was aged, savage, mean and grim;
That baron Breuse, the Heartless, lived with him,
Of all bad men the worst;
That in Tintagel, nest-rock of the mew,
His daughters lived with him, the dark Ygraine,
That moon of women; then the bright Elaine,
And little Morgause, whom a witch had curst.

So, knowing that the urger of a cause
Must urge the cause in person, Uther rode
With Kol and Guy, to Merchyon's abode,
And in Tintagel tower
Pled eloquently to him without pause,
With all a young man's beauty, flusht and true;
And as he pled, Ygerna watcht, and knew
That of all knights Prince Uther was the flower.

Then Merchyon answered, 'I have heard your plea.
I will not mingle in remote affairs,
I can mind mine, let others manage theirs:
What can the East, or Wales,
Or all of northern Britain, mean to me?
No Cornish men shall bleed in the employ
Of you, or others like you, Roman boy.
Your schemes are childish and your fears are tales.

Or if not so, perhaps the Romans plan
To recommence their empire, for in truth
Taxes and tribute and conscripted youth
Are playthings dear to Rome.
But you, my Roman, come to the wrong man.'
So raging, wrapping close his scarlet cloak,
He left the hall: Breuse, as he followed, spoke.
'That was your answer, Uther; make for home.'

Breuse and his sworders followed Merchyon out,
Uther had neither welcome nor farewell,
Comfort, nor rest, nor water from the well,
Nor food for man or horse.
He stood a moment, betwixt rage and doubt.
'Sir,' said Ygerna, coming from her place,
'Father is old: forgive his want of grace.
To-morrow he'll be broken with remorse.'

Then Uther for the first time saw Ygern;
And at her voice and at her wistful glance,
Love stabbed his spirit with her beauty's lance;
While she, made faint with love,
Felt the hot blush upon her temples burn.
Love to both startled mortals made it known
That each was other's to the inward bone
Through some old passion in the stars above.

As in October when the Channel mist
With silent swathes of greyness hides the sea
Until none knows where land or waters be,
And suddenly a blast
Scatters and shreds the vapours into twist
And all is glorious sunlight, wind and foam,
Through which a towering ship comes striding home,
Spray to the rail, with colours at her mast;

Or as, in mild Novembers, when the pack
Whimpers in covert and the hunters wait,
Under slow-dropping oak-leaves falling late,
Making no sound at all,
And suddenly the fox with hollow back
Breaks, with a crying leader at his brush,
And all those riders gathered for the rush
Surge for the fence, not heeding any call;

So, to those two, the greyness and delay
Of all their lives' endeavour and employ,
The hollowness which they had counted joy,
The hopes which had been dear
Until that instant, all were swept away;
They were alone upon an ocean shore
Where nothing meant nor mattered any more
Save their two souls and being without fear.

'O Princess,' he began, 'O dark-haired Queen,
O moon of women, we have met again,
We who are one yet have been cut atwain
To seek ourselves till now.
Whatever griefs are coming or have been,
Love in his glory grants us to make whole
Our bleeding portions of divided soul
That our last dying sundered with the plough.'

And she replied, 'Even as a winter bird,
Robin or chaffinch, in the iron day
Mopes, with pufft feathers, on the snowy spray,
Too pincht with cold to fly,
Too starved with bitter need to sing a word,
Till, from the farm, maid Gillian scatters crumbs,
And the bird, gladdened, knows that April comes
And carols his thanksgiving, so am I.'

Then, being in the certainty of love,
That cannot doubt, however it be blind,
Those two young lovers plighted mind to mind,
And straightway told the King;
Who cried, 'A pretty plot, by Heaven above.
Since I, as King, refused to be allied,
You think to win my power through a bride
Whose loving father grants her everything.

Not so, my Roman, for I see your plot.
Keep to your own princesses; she shall wed
My Breuse, who has no Latin in his head,
And you shall go out shamed…
You sworders, make this loving swain less hot…
Set him ahorseback with his head for home.
And keep from Cornwall henceforth, man of Rome,
Or Cornish hands will swiftly have you tamed.'

Then instantly, before Ygraine could plead,
Or Uther answer, he was hustled forth
(He and his Knights) and headed for the north,
With orders not to turn.
Since three alone were helpless, they agreed
To the tide's setting, but they rode in rage,
Vowing to set King Merchyon in a cage
Next Sarum Fair, to suffer and to learn.

Yet, after noon, as Uther stayed to look
West, from the moorland, at Ygerna's home,
There, on the moor, he saw a horseman come
Black against burning sky,
Galloping tow'rds him, by the way he took.
And being near, behold, it was Elaine,
Flusht, tousled, riding on a tautened rein,
Calling, 'O Uther, help, or she will die...

Help us to-night, because my Father swears
That Breuse shall wed Ygerna before Prime...
Friend, can you help her in so little time?...
Not let her go to Breuse...'
'Men have plucked women out of dragons' lairs,'
King Uther said, 'And I will pluck Ygraine.
O Rose in briars difficult to gain,
Lighten my mind with strategems to use.'

Then, having thought, he said, 'This seems a chance.
Your porter's old: suppose I climb the rock,
Dresst like the King your father, and then knock
At midnight on the door.
He, being old and drowsy, may but glance,
Think me your father, bow, and open gates,
Then, when I bring Ygern from where she waits,
He may unfasten for me as before.

It is worth trying, for, if it succeed,
Ygern and I will be beyond the wall;
And I can see no other chance at all
Of saving her to-night...
And if I save her, sister, as God speed,
I swear to take her to the hermit's cell
And marry her before we cross the fell,
Making her Queen from Isis to the Wight.

You, Kol and Guy, arrange for horse-relays,
From here to where King Merchyon's country ends;
Swift horses, mind. About it: gallop, friends:
And if the luck be fair,
We'll meet again in Sarum in three days.
Sister, be ready when the moon goes west.
The hermit knows me, he is Bran the Blest,
He will assist us: have the horses there.'

* * * *

Who longs for time to pass? The child at school,
Sick for his home where understandings dwell;
He who counts tiles within a prison-cell;
The broken, with her wrongs;
Eagles in cages stared at by the fool;
To all these dreary longers, at the last,
Some bell of blessing tells *the hour is past*:
But none longs for it as the lover longs.

Still, at the last, to Uther, the sun dimmed;
Men drew old sails across the half-built ricks;
The quarrymen trudged home with shouldered picks;
Slow-footed cows turned home;
After the chapel-bell ceast, voices hymned;
Evening came quiet: all the world had turned
To rest and supper where the rushlights burned:
Tintagel blackened like a dragon's comb.

By moonlight Uther came to Bran the Blest
Whose shed now held the horses of Elaine,
Bold-eyed, high-mettled, leaners on the rein,
Waiting their King and Queen.
At moonset, helped by Bran, Prince Uther dresst
With crown and scarlet and a sheep's-wool beard
Like Merchyon's self; then down he went, and neared
The rock-cut stairway slimy with sea-green.

He clambered up, while far above his head,
Black on the sky, the battlements were grim;
The sentries paced above, not seeing him,
Nor hearing how he climbed.
Beneath, within the bay, the ripples spread
One after other slowly to the shore,
Where, gleaming but unbroken, they gave o'er
Like breathing from a sleeper, husht and timed.

Upon the topmost stair he stood intent
Outside the gate, to listen, while the feet
Of drowsy sentries passed upon their beat.
He heard, beyond the door,
The porter, breathing deeply where he leant
Sprawled over table near the charcoal pan.
'Come, courage,' thought Prince Uther, 'play the man.'
He knocked King Merchyon's knocking and gave o'er.

As he had hoped, he heard the porter rouse,
Garble some words, unhook the lantern-ring,
Kick back the bench, and mutter, 'It's the King!'
Then fumble on the bar,
Pulling it weakly, gulping down his drowse.
The oaken barbolt loitered slowly back,
The latchet clicked, light yellowed at the crack,
An old man louted with the door ajar.

And as he louted low, Prince Uther passt…
There was Elaine, to take him to Ygern,
Telling the porter to expect return
Within few moments more.
All ways are long to lovers, but at last
He found Ygerna waiting in the dim,
Her great eyes bright, her white arms stretcht to him;
He drew her back along the corridor.

They trod the dark stone passage between rooms
Where people slept beneath the sentry's tread;
Tintagel seemed a castle of the dead.
A horse-hoof scraped the stone
Where the King's stallion waked among the grooms.
The porter, with his old eyes full of sleep,
Opened the gate to let them from the keep;
Its clang behind them thrilled them to the bone.

They crept like spies adown the cragside stair,
Into the gully's blackness between crags;
They heard the spear-butts clang upon the flags
At changing of the guard.
No challenge came: the world was unaware
How lovers fled: they reached the castle brook
Where every-changing gleaming ever shook
An image of the zenith many-starred.

No sentry saw them; no one challenged; no,
Not when they moved across the moorland crest
Leaving the castle black against the west,
Grim guardian of the sea.
Their footsteps made a drowsy cock to crow,
A dog barked at their passing by the farm,
But no one stirred nor answered the alarm:
They reached the hermit's chapel: they were free.

There in the little chapel of the well,
By taper-light, the hermit made them one.
'Now cross the moor,' he said, 'before the sun.
God be your guard and speed.'
They turned the chafing horses to the fell,
That King and bride upon their marriage day;
The nightingale still sang upon the spray,
The glow-worm's lamp still burned among the weed.

All day and night they hurried from pursuit;
Next morning found them out of Merchyon's land
Beside a brook with wood on either hand,
Deep in a dell of green:
Cool water wrinkled at the flag-flower-root,
The meadowsweet her heavy fragrance shed:
'Here,' the pair thought, 'shall be our marriage bed,
Here, in this orchard of the fairy queen.'

So there they halted in the summer flowers,
The speedwell blue, the stitchwort starry bright,
The dog-rose not yet opened, pink or white,
But sweet as very love.
Blackbirds and thrushes sang the lovers' hours,
And when the young moon brightened golden-pale
In the blue heaven, lo, a nightingale
Singing her heart out on the spray above.

There the two loved. Alas! ere morning came,
There Breuse and Merchyon, finding them asleep,
Stabbed Uther dead, and took Ygern to weep
In grim Tintagel tower.
There she sat weeping at the weaving-frame,
Waiting to bear her son before she died;
And as she wept, poor woman, hollow-eyed,
She wove the story of her happy hour:–

The creeping from the castle in the dark,
The blinking porter drowsed in lantern light,
The hermit and the chapel and the rite,
The horses tried and true;
Dawn on the moorland with the singing lark,
The ride for safety ever glancing round;
Then the sweet loving place, where they were found
At dawn among the speedwell in the dew.

And sometimes Merchyon, mindful of his girl,
In mercy of her health, would have her ta'en
To rest beside the Alan with Elaine,
Guarded by Breuse's band.
There as she watcht the water-eddies whirl,
Often a dark-eyed deer with fawn at heel,
Would shyly nuzzle her to share her meal,
And robin redbreasts percht upon her hand.

Midsummer Night

Midsummer night had fallen at full moon,
So, being weary of my ancient tale,
I turned into the night,
Up the old trackway leading from the vale.
The downland dimmed before me, dune on dune,
Pale dogrose buds about me shed their scent;
The startled peewits glimmered as they went,
The moonlight made the earth and heaven white;
The heaven and earth together uttered June.

So perfect was the beauty, that the air
Was like immortal presence thrilling all
The downland with deep life;
Presences communed in the white owl's call;
The rampart of the hill-top stood up bare,
High on the windy hill a brightness shone –
I wondered whose, since shepherd-men had gone
Homeward a long time since to food and wife;
Yet brightness shone, as from a lantern there.

Then, as the valley belfries chimed the hour,
I thought: 'On summer nights King Arthur's door,
By yonder sarsens shut,
Is said to open to a corridor
Hewn far within the hill to Arthur's bower,
Where he and Gwenivere, with all the tale
Of captains toughened by the weight of mail,
Bide in a hall within the limestone cut:
That is the doorway, this is Arthur's hour.'

So, pressing near, behold, a door was wide
Flung open on the steepness of the hill,
Showing a lighted shaft.
A footlift fox was paused upon the sill;
Eyes gleaming green, he fled. I stepped inside.
The passage led within all brightly lit,
Deft limestone hewers' hands had fashioned it.
Behind me (as I thought) the white owl laught.
The lighted way before me was my guide.

Till deep within the hill, I reacht a hall
Lit, but so vast that all aloft was dim.
The chivalry below
Sat at their table stirring not a limb.
Even as frost arrests the waterfall,
So had a power frozen that array,
There at the banquet of the holy day,
Into such stillness that I could not know
If they were dead, or carved, or living all.

Then, entering in, accustomed to the light,
I marked them well: King Arthur, black and keen,
Pale, eager, wise, intense;
Lime-blossom Gwenivere, the red-gold queen;
Ban's son, the kingly, Lancelot the bright;
Gawaine, Bors, Hector; all whom trumpets drew
Up Badon at the falling of the dew:
And over them there brooded the immense
Helper or Spirit with immortal sight.

All was most silent in that cavern nave
Save a far water dripping, drop by drop,
In some dark way of time.
Power had brought that Knighthood to a stop,
Not even their ragged banners seemed to wave,
No whisper stirred the muscle of a cheek,
Yet all seemed waiting for the King to speak.
Far, far below I heard the midnight chime,
The valley bells that buried silence clave.

Then, at that distant music Arthur stirred;
His scarlet mantle quivered like a wing.
Each, in his golden stall,
Smiling a little, turned towards the King,
Who from his throne of glory spoke this word:–
'Midsummer Night permits us to declare
How Nature's sickle cut us from the air
And made the splendour of our summer fall.'
Then one by one they answered as I heard.

KING ARTHUR:
'I was the cause of the disastrous end...
I in my early manhood sowed the seed
That made the Kingdom rend.
I begot Modred in my young man's greed.
When the hot blood betrays us, who gives heed?
Morgause and I were lovers for a night,
Not knowing how the fates had made us kin.
So came the sword to smite,
So was the weapon whetted that made bleed:
That young man's loving let the ruin in.'

GWENIVERE:
'I, Gwenivere the Queen, destroyed the realm;
I, by my love of Lancelot the Bright;
Destiny being strong and mortals weak,
And women loving as the summer night.
When I was seized by Kolgrim Dragon Helm,
Lancelot saved me from the Dragon-beak,
Love for my saviour came to overwhelm.

Too well I loved him, for my only son,
Lacheu, was his, not Arthur's as men thought.
I longed to see my lover's son the King;
But Lacheu, riding into Wales, was caught
By pirates near St David's and undone...
They killed my Lacheu there.
The primroses of spring,
Red with his blood, were scattered in his hair:
Thereafter nothing mattered to me aught...

Save Lancelot perhaps at bitter whiles,
When the long pain was more than I could stand;
He being Arthur's cousin, was his heir
Till base-born Modred reacht us from the isles.
Thereafter was no comfort anywhere,
But Modred's plottings and my sister's wiles,
And love that lit me ruining the land.'

LANCELOT:
'I, who am Lancelot, the son of Ban,
King Arthur's cousin, dealt the land the blow
From which the griefs began.
I, who loved Gwenivere, as all men know,
Was primal cause that brought the kingdom low,
For all was peace until that quarrel fell;
Thereafter red destruction followed fast.
The gates of hell
Hedge every daily track by which men go;
My loving flung them open as I passt.'

GWENIVACH:
'I, who am Princess Gwenivach the Fair,
Compasst the kingdom's ruin by my hate,
The poisonous hate I bare
For Gwenivere, my sister, Arthur's mate.
My mind was as a murderer in wait
Behind a door, on tiptoe, with a knife,
Ready to stab her at the slightest chance,
Stab to the life.
I stabbed her to the heart in her estate;
Disaster was my blow's inheritance.'

145

MODRED:

'Not you, with your begettings, father mine;
Not you, my red-gold Queen, adultress proud;
Not you, Sir Lancelot, whom none could beat;
Not you, my princess sweet;
Not one of all you waters was worth wine.
Mine was the hand that smote this royal seat,
Mine was the moving darkness that made cloud;
You were but nerves; I, Modred, was the spine.

You were poor puppets in a master's game;
I, Modred, was the cause of what befell.
I, Modred, Arthur's bastard, schemed and planned;
I, with my single hand,
Gave but a touch, and, lo, the troubles came;
And royalty was ended in the land.
When shut from Heaven, devils create hell:
Those who ignore this shall repent the same.

You were at peace, King Arthur (cuckold's peace);
Your queen had both her lover and her son;
And I, your bastard by your aunt, was far,
Where Orkney tide-rips jar.
Your Kingdom was all golden with increase.
Then your son's killing happened: Modred's star
Rose; I was heir, my bastardy was done;
Or (with more truth) I swore to make it cease.

But coming to your court with double claim
(As son and nephew) to the British crown,
You and the Queen named Lancelot the heir;
A brave man and a rare;
Your cousin King, the cuckoo to your dame,
Whom nobody opposed till I was there.
But I opposed, until I tumbled down
The realm to ruin and the Queen to shame.'

GWENIVACH TO GWENIVERE:
'And I, your younger sister, whom you slighted,
Loved Modred from the first and took his part.
That made the milk of your sweet fortune sour.
I told you in the tower,
The green-hung tower, by the sunset lighted,
Sunset and moonrise falling the same hour;
Then I declared how Modred had my heart,
That we were lovers, that our troths were plighted.

You could have won our love, had you been wise;
Then, when, as lovers, we confesst and pled
Together with you for a lasting truce.
No blood would have been shed,
April and June had had their natural use,
And autumn come with brimming granaries.
But no; you gave refusal and abuse;
Therefore I smote your lips so harlot-red...
The joy of that one buffet never dies.

I see you at this moment, standing still,
White, by the window in that green-hung tower,
Just as I struck you, while your great eyes gleamed.
Till then, I had but seemed...
My striking showed you how I longed to kill.
O through what years of insult had I dreamed
For that one stroke in the avenging hour!
The devil of my hatred had her will:
God pity me, fate fell not as I deemed.'

So, with lamenting of the ancient woe
They told their playings in the tragic plot,
Until their eyes were bright:
The red-gold beauty wept for Lancelot.
Then the church belfries in the vale below
Chimed the first hour of the year's decay,
And Arthur spoke: 'Our hour glides away;
Gone is the dim perfection of the night,
Not yet does any trumpet bid us go.

But when the trumpet summons, we will rise,
We, who are fibres of the country's soul,
We will take horse and come
To purge the blot and make the broken whole;
And make a green abundance seem more wise,
And build the lasting beauty left unbuilt
Because of all the follies of our guilt.
But now the belfry chimes us to be dumb,
Colour is coming in the eastern skies.'

Then as those figures lapsed again to stone,
The horses stamped, the cock his challenge flung,
The gold-wrought banners stirred,
The air was trembling from the belfry's tongue.
Above those forms the Helper stood alone,
Shining with hope. But now the dew was falling,
In unseen downland roosts the cocks were calling,
And dogrose petals shaken by a bird
Dropped from the blossomed briar and were strown.

Dust to Dust

Henry Plantagenet, the English King,
Came with Fair Rosamond, for monkish picks
Had lifted flaggings set in Roman bricks
And cleared a Latin-carven slab which told
That Arthur and his Queen were buried there...

They watched: the diggers raised the covering...
There lay those great ones placid under pyx;
Arthur enswathed as by a burning wing
Or wave of Gwenivere's undying hair,
Which lit the vaulty darkness with its gold.

Seeing such peace the living lovers knelt
And sought each other's hands: those dead ones lay
Untouched by any semblance of decay,
Liker to things immortal than things dead,
Manhood's undying glory, beauty's queen.

The crimson rose in Rosamunda's belt
Dropped, on the dead, one petal, soft as may.
Like ice that unseen April makes to melt,
Those bodies ceast, as though they had not been;
The petal lay on powder within lead.

from Any Dead to Any Living

Any Dead to Any Living

Boast not about our score.
Think this: – There was no need
For such a Sack of Youth
As burned our lives.
We, and the millions more,
Were Waste, from want of heed,
From world-wide hate of truth,
And souls in gyves.

Let the dead bury the dead.
Let the great graveyard be.
Life had not health to climb,
It loved no strength that saves.
Furbish our million graves
As records of a crime;
But give our brothers bread,
Unfetter heart and head,
Set prisoned angels free.

Miscellaneous Verse, 1922–1930

The Racer

I saw the racer coming to the jump
Staring with fiery eyeballs as he rusht;
I heard the blood within his body thump,
I saw him launch, I heard the toppings crusht.

And as he landed I beheld his soul
Kindle, because, in front, he saw the Straight
With all its thousands roaring at the goal;
He laughed, he took the moment for his mate.

Would that the passionate moods on which we ride
Might kindle thus to one-ness with the will;
Would we might see the end to which we stride,
And feel, not strain in struggle, only thrill,

And laugh like him to know in all our nerves
Beauty, the spirit, scattering dust and turves.

[*The Racer* ([Oxford: John Masefield, 1922]); privately printed
poetry card]

St Felix School

Here, in this house, where we are singing thus,
Long generations will come after us.
Friends we shall never know will come to share
This life of ours, wondering what we were;
Long after we are gone their minds will take
The human pathways our endeavours make:
We shall not see them; but we can endow
This place with beauty for them, here and now.
We can so live that after we are dead

They may find beauty here like daily bread.
We can so live that they may find, each one
A life here of truth said and kindness done;
The knowledge, that this world of mysteries
Wants many thousands true for one that's wise;
The faith, that when a twilight finds us gone,
All we have consecrated will live on
To help the souls of other unseen friends
Into a calm where beauty never ends.

[*St Felix School Southwold 1897–1923* (London: Chelsea Publishing
Co. [1923]), p. 5]

['On these three things a poet must depend…']

On these three things a poet must depend
His Will, his Natural Talent and his Friend.

Bitter, though honour is it, if he do
Aught with the first without the other two.

Happy, but impotent, however stirred,
The second is without the first and third.

Untoucht, unprized, like water without thirst
The third must be sans second and sans first.

And often two combine, yet, lacking one,
The light is of the moon not of the sun.

Yet when the Trinity exults, oh, then
What bliss to be, although despised of men.

[HRHRC. MS (Masefield, J.) Works [Untitled poem] 'On these three
things a poet must depend…']

Lines on Sea Adventure

I saw the old, rust-spotted, ill-found ship
Pass through the dock-gates on another quest.
The hurry of the river made her dip
So that its darkness whitened at her breast.

A band of men (too few) bent at her bows
Getting her anchors inboard before dark;
I heard them sing a song like a carouse;
I watched her light die down into a spark.

I thought that thus, these seven hundred years,
Our ships have gone where never pathway showed
Manned by the hope that never yields to fears
To wander the unknown and find a road

And bring, to some lone farm in Kent or Devon,
'Some crownes, some spoiles, a little dew of Heaven.'

Thus they have gone; but far from sight of land
Or other eye than theirs, what have they known,
What miracles of courage and of hand
When all salvation failed them save their own?

What miseries of fire, and frost, and thirst,
Fever and pestilence, and stroke of sun?
What Acts of God destroying the accurst?
What acts of man, slaughter and malison?

What chance, of the wind holding or tide failing
What luck, of shift of current here or here,
What awe, of the berg's ghost above the railing
Or of the breaker's wraith a fathom clear.

What terror of the toppling sea that towers,
Then whelms, as hers, the manhood that was ours?

If some among those men were hot for gain
As pirates on the sea, or for the spoil
Of seaport cities on the Spanish Main,
Or to snatch negroes to a life of toil,

These were the few, the many, with hard hands
Dragged, boated, hoisted, stowed the bargained freight,
Chaffered in all the tongues of foreign lands,
Starved, thirsted, froze, went sleepless, early, late;

Died young, unknown, yet from their countless pains
Wrought this, that still abides, a charted sea,
A world made little wherein conquering brains
Can pass from land to new land, setting free,

Freeing this soul of man that in its cage
Turns, and is weary of it, age by age.

[Basil Lubbock, *Adventures by Sea from Art of Old Time* (London:
The Studio, 1925), pp. 1–3]

Polyxena's Speech

From the Hecuba of Euripides

I see you, Odysseus, hiding your right hand
Under your cloak, and turning round your face
Lest I should touch your beard. Be of good Courage
You have escaped from God, that pleader for me.
Be sure that I will follow, since I must,
And since I wish it. If I did not wish,
I should seem a spotted girl and a life-clinger.

What urge have I to live? My father was the king
Of all the Phrygians at my first beginnings.
Then I was brought up under noble hopes
As a king's bride: there was no little rivalry
To what king's hearth and household I should come.
I, the unhappy one, was leader then,
Of all the girls of Ida the most gazed at,
God's equal, save for death. Now I am slave.

The name alone makes me to long for death.
I am not used to it.

Next, I may chance on brutal-hearted masters,
And one may buy me for silver – I, the sister
Of Hector and of many other princes –
Who will force me to bread-kneading in his house,
To sweeping house, and standing, beating the loom-sword,
Harshly compelled to endure bitter days.
Then some bought bond-slave will defile my bed,
I, who was formerly thought worthy princes.
No, never.
I will give up with free light in my eyes,
And consecrate my body unto death.

So lead me, Odysseus, even to my act of death.
I see no likelihood nor any hope
Of good things coming to give courage to me.
Do not stop me, mother, not by word nor deed.
Agree that I shall die, ere shameful things come.

One, not accustomed to bear evils, suffers
Having the neck in yoke.
To die may be far happier than life,
For life not beautiful is a great burden.

O my beloved mother, give me now
Your sweetest hand, and kiss me cheek to cheek,
Since never again, but now, for the last time,
I am to see the sun and the sun's light.
Take these my last words at my ending, mother.
O mother mine, I am going down to death.
O Light,
It is still fitting that I cry your name,
Although I share you but for so much time
As lets me reach the sword-edge and the pyre.

[*The Oxford Recitations* (New York: Macmillan Company, 1928),
pp. 47–9]

1930–1967

from The Wanderer of Liverpool

Adventure On

Adventure on, companion, for this
Is God's most greatest gift, the thing that is.
Take it, although it lead to the abyss.

Go forth to seek: the quarry never found
Is still a fever to the questing hound,
The skyline is a promise, not a bound.

Therefore, go forth, companion: when you find
No highway more, no track, all being blind
The way to go shall glimmer in the mind.

Though you have conquered Earth and charted Sea
And planned the courses of all Stars that be,
Adventure on, more wonders are in Thee.

Adventure on, for from the littlest clue
Has come whatever worth man ever knew;
The next to lighten all men may be you.

Adventure on, and if you suffer, swear
That the next venturer shall have less to bear;
Your way will be retrodden, make it fair.

Think, though you thunder on in might, in pride,
Others may follow fainting, without guide,
Burn out a trackway for them; blaze it wide.

Only one banner, Hope: only one star
To steer by, Hope, a dim one seen afar
Yet naught will vanquish Hope and nothing bar.

Your Hope is what you venture for, your Hope
Is but the shadowed semblance of your scope,
The chink of gleaming towards which you grope.

What though the gleam be but a feeble one,
Go on, the man behind you may have none;
Even the dimmest gleam is from the sun.

Be very sure, that good things truly willed
Survive the broken heart, the martyr killed,
Hope that endures becomes a Hope fulfilled.

Liverpool, 1890

Gray sea dim, smoke-blowing, hammer-racket, sirens
Calling from ships, ear-breaking riveting, the calthrops
Of great gray drays, fire-smiting on the cobbles, dragging
The bales of cotton.

The warehouse roofs, wet-gleaming, the ships bedraggled
Awry-swung yards, backt on the main, the jib booms
Run in, the winches clanking, the slings of cargo
Running up, jolt.

There lie the ships, paint-rusted, each as a person
In rake or sheer or rig, coulters or counters,
Sea-shearing bows, those swords of beauty that thrust
The heart with rapture.

All fair ships, man-killers some, sea-eagles, sluggards.
Tall, too, many: lofty, a dread to look at, dizzy thus:
Among them always one more sky-aspiring, queen,
Remembered always.

Liverpool, 1930

The dockyards of the ancient days are filled
With roads and buildings: of the ships that were
Not any lift their glory to the air;
The singing of their coming-in is stilled.

All has become much greater than of old,
Man has advanced in mastery afar,
The soul of man is conquering his star,
Mud has been changed for granite, dross for gold.

O Capital, whose highway is the sea,
I think of forty years hence, when your spires
Will flame with beauty's intellectual fires,
And what your sons imagine now, will be.

Pay

The world paid but a penny for its toil,
That which was priceless got the beggar's dole;
Men who fetcht beauty, iron, corn or oil
Scarce could keep beggar's bones about the soul.

I saw those sailing seamen, cotton-clad,
Housed in wet kennels, worm-fed, cheated, driven,
Three pounds a month, and small delight they had,
Save the bright water and the winds of heaven.

Yet from their sweated strength an order rose
The full-rigged ship in her delightful line
So beautiful and tranquil in repose
But in supremest action so divine.

For in the trampling seas the beauty stood
Trampling those seas, and made her pathway good.

Eight Bells

Four double strokes repeated on the bells,
And then away, away the shufflers go
Aft to the darkness where the ruler dwells,
Where by the rail he sucks his pipe aglow;
Beside him his relief looks down on those below.

There in the dark they answer to their names,
Those dozen men, and one relieves the wheel,
One the look-out, the others sit to games
In moonlight, backed against the bulkhead's steel,
In the lit patch the hands flick, card by card, the deal.

Meanwhile the men relieved are forward all,
Some in their bunks asleep, while others sing
Low-voiced some ditty of the halliard-fall,
The ship impels them on with stooping wing,
Rolling and roaring on with triumph in her swing.

Posted

Dream after dream I see the wrecks that lie
Unknown of man, unmarked upon the charts,
Known of the flat-fish with the withered eye,
And seen by women in their aching hearts.

World-wide the scattering is of those fair ships
That trod the billow tops till out of sight:
The cuttle mumbles them with horny lips
The shells of the sea-insects crust them white.

In silence and in dimness and in greenness
Among the indistinct and leathery leaves
Of fruitless life they lie among the cleanness.
Fish glide and flit, slow under-movement heaves:

But no sound penetrates, not even the lunge
Of live ships passing, nor the gannet's plunge.

If

If it could be, that in this southern port
They should return upon the south-west gale
To make again the empty bay their court
Queen beyond queen, at rest or under sail.

And if, from every ship, the songs should rise
From those strong throats, and all be as before,
Should we not all be changed and recognize
Their inner power and exalt them more?

Not so, we should not, we should let them be,
Each age must have its unregarded use,
That is but of its time, on land and sea,
Things have their moment, not a longer truce.

Each darkness has her stars, and when each sets
The dawn, that hardly saw her, soon forgets.

Son of Adam

Once on a time there was a lusty Lion
Just come of age, within the Libyan desert,
A handsome he, all shiny with manly beauty.

So on his coming-of-age-day out he went
Forth from his father's palace, caring no straw
For how his Mother beggd him to be careful:
For 'Oh,' she cried, out of the palace turret,
'Beware, my lovely boy, of Son of Adam.
Of all the dangerous deadly beasts of Earth,
He is the dangerousest and the deadliest.'

This shiny Lion, full of beauty of youth,
Went to the drinking-pools where the gazelles went,
But not to seek gazelles. Into the water
He peered a long, long time at his reflection,
And smiled and said: 'Perhaps not beautiful,
But oh, how interesting and how virile.
Let Son of Adam come here: only let him.'
Then, rising up, he pac't into the desert
Shewing his teeth, lashing his flank with his tail,
And with deep coughing roars calling aloud
'Come, Son of Adam, with your deadly danger.'

And lo, out of the air there came a stranger,
A grey bird ghastly, with all tail feathers gone,
Part pluckt, part moulted, altogether batterd.

'What Animal are you?' the Lion askt it.

'I'm a Goose Animal,' the creature answerd.
'And I am running away from Son of Adam
Who longs to cook and eat me: he has ravisht
My feathers, as you see: it is his custom
To eat us geese with apple sauce and sages;
Our feathers stuff his beds, our grease, out-melted,

He rubs upon his skin to make him shiny.
He is a deadly thing, the Son of Adam.'

The Lion answer'd: 'Leave the matter to Me.
Myself will deal with him and see you righted.'

He pac't a little further upon his way
And lo, another creature, witherd and gray,
Came hobbling, stumbling, ribbed and shoulder-sorry
A lop-eared, pondering thing, clever, perverse.

'What Animal are you?' the Lion askt it.

'I am a Donkey Animal,' it answerd.
'And I am running away from Son of Adam.
Who bangs me with a stick and makes me labour
Dragging the load of barley sacks to market,
Beatings and kicks and curses are my portion,
The chaff the horses leave, the hay the cows leave,
The meal the pigs refuse, and autumn wind-falls:
These, and, sometimes, a happy dream of carrots.
A dream, I say, a vision, that on waking
Fades to an empty crib with the rain dripping.

Such is my life, but even when pale Death comes
To end my life of sorrows and release me
Still Son of Adam comes, he takes my skin off
And moulds it into what he knows as vellum
On which his devilish deep ones write their deeds.
Dangerous are the deeds of Son of Adam.'

'Leave him to me, my friend,' the Lion answerd,
'Myself will deal with him and see you righted.'

Onwards he pac't, engrosst in his importance,
And as he felt the wiseness of his wisdom,
Lo, coming thither was another creature
A little like the Donkey in his feature
But shorter in the ear and sadder-looking
The ribs more staring and the knees more broken
Such as a cats'-meat man would rub his hands at.

'What Animal are *you?*' the Lion askt it.

'I am a Pack-Horse Animal,' it answered.
'And I am running away from Son of Adam.
Deadly and dangerous is Son of Adam:
He makes my life a burden beyond bearing,
With ploughing, harrowing and homing harvest,
Taking the sacks to mill, turning the mill-stone,
Then dragging back the flour to the baker.
And always being ridden, having my jaw jabb'd
With snatchings on the bit and "Back there, will you."
And always getting saddle-galls and spavins
And curby hocks and colic and the staggers.
And for my food, to give me strength to labour
I ask you what, and Echo answers with me.
Chaff that a sailor would reject in biscuit;
Hay that a politician would not purchase
During a war, and corn the forage merchants
Could not dispose of, even to a general.
And in the green time, in the happy summer,
When the pink clover blossoms in the hayfield,
And all beasts banquet, never think that I do,
Not with a Son of Adam for a master
I snatch a dusty mouthful from the roadside
The while I drag the hayload to the hayrick
And even then am struck, and Son of Adam
Cries, "You're not here to gormandize but labour.
Pull up, now, to your collar; pull, you cab-horse."

And even when I perish, Son of Adam
Makes profit of me, selling me to kennels
To boil with barley into broth for foxhounds,
And others boil my horny hoofs for jelly
And sell my flesh for cats'-meat or for sausage;
Unhappy Pack-Horse, deadly Son of Adam.'

'Leave him to me, my friend,' the Lion answerd.
'Myself will deal with him and see you righted.'

So, pacing on, he mus'd, 'In after ages
These paltry beasts will raise a temple to me,
The Lion of all Lions of all Lions
Loud roaring vanquisher of Son of Adam,
Where is this Son of Adam? Let me see him.'

And as he spoke, behold, coming towards him,
There was a Something of a mildewed aspect
So sorrowful, so furless and so feeble
That it was doubtful what it could be reckon'd;
Whether an Animal or only Nightmare.

It had no teeth to speak of, and no talons,
No fur upon its head, but moulted baldness,
Two wretched legs it had, and one a lame one,
A coat all ragged, shewing rags beneath it.
Across its back was slung a builder's wallet
And on its shoulders, staggeringly, it bore
A load of planks and also an iron door.

And seeing it, at first, the Lion doubted
Whether to stoop to speak to such a creature.
Then with extreme misliking and disfavour
He askt the thing: 'What Animal are you then?'

The creature, putting down his burdens, panted
And toucht his brow, and said, 'To tell the truth, sir,
I am a Builder Animal, so please you.
And I am running away from Son of Adam,
Because I can't agree with Son of Adam.
And why? Because this Son of Adam asks me
To build at things I cannot reckon building.
They are not building, no, but jerry-building,
These bungalows in ribbons down a roadside,
These cottages constructed by the Council,
Workers like me can't reckon them as building.
Give me to build at building that *is* building;
One of these towers like a minaret now
Or pyramid all pointed for a Pharaoh…

But tripe, not taste, is Son of Adam's fancy.
No use to talk to him of architecture
Besides he wants no workers, no, but wage-slaves
That he can grind to do his deeds of darkness.
I tell him plain I'll do no jerry-building...
Since Builder-Animals must die like others,
I say "Die building palaces not pigsties."
So here I come, to build a palace, *and* die.'
Salt tears were glistening in the Builder's eye.
'I come,' he said, 'prepard to build a palace
For him they call the King of Beasts, the Monarch
Of all live things, the Conqueror and Captain
The Emperor of Animals, The Leopard.'

'Leopard?' the Lion said, 'You are mistaken.
The Leopard is not Emperor nor Captain,
Nor Conqueror, not Monarch; he is nothing...
The certain spotty grace that we accord him
He shares with currant dumplings and hyænas...
And as for King, he's less a King than you are.
Lions have palaces and leopards lairs, sir...
And that if Lions choose. I am a Lion...
Build me a palace: talk no more of Leopards...
For by the Lion Sun who ranges Heaven
Tossing his mane of fire from his shoulders,
To talk of Leopards in such terms is treason.'

'Forgive me my mistake, sir,' said the Builder.
'It comes from all that Son of Adam taught me.
Leopards indeed! Indeed I see my error,
Seeing a royal Lion like yourself, sir,
(That is, as far as I can see, from dazzle).
O what great joy and rapture and promotion
For this poor wage slave 'scapt from Son of Adam
To build a palace for a Royal Lion
A Conqueror and Emperor and Sultan.
To think that with these plankings and this hammer
These hands will build a palace for your Kingship
To see your smiles and echo with your singing
And gleam with the reflection of your beauty.
For, Sir, when I beheld your beauty coming

I thought, "This is some planet or some angel."
And now, to think I am to build your palace.
O happy Builder-Animal, thrice happy:
O lucky nails, O blessed plank and hammer.'

And as he spoke, he built a little palace
Then turnd it upside down, and through the bottom
Drove four and five inch nails, so that the points stuck
Up, through the floors, and each one pointing inward.

'Why drive the nails like that?' the Lion askt him.
'In royal palaces we always put them,'
The builder said, 'It is the royal hall mark.
The palace is now ready, if it please you.
Will you walk in?'

'It is not very big,' the Lion answerd.
'There's lots of room inside, I do assure you,'
The Builder said, 'As sweet a little palace
Ay, and as roomy as a King could look for.
Just step inside and see it for yourself, sir.'

So stooping down the Lion crawled within it,
And instantly the Builder clapped the door to,
The iron door, and lockt it with a padlock.
Then went away, but soon returned rejoicing
Riding the Donkey Animal, and plucking
The Goose for dinner, while he drove the Pack-Horse.

He halted there, and hove the Lion palace
The Lion still inside, onto the Pack-Horse
And drove him to the Sultan, where he sold him.

from A Tale of Troy

The Horse

My Father, King Epeios of the Islands,
Fashioned the Horse, after Odysseus' plan.
His shipwrights helped: this was the fashion of it:

The body of the horse was a hooped hollow
Of staves of wood, shaped to the horse's shape.
Within it, on each side, and at the chest
Were seats, covered with fleeces against noise,
To take five men, close-sitting two a side
Bent forward somewhat, and the fifth at end
Who sat more upright since his head had space
Within the horse's neck.
                          The entry hatch
Was in the beast's back, bolted from within
And covered with a saddle-piece of gold.

All this was made most secretly, unknown
By any, save Odysseus and my Father,
Who worked in a locked hut, under a guard,
'The work,' they said, 'being consecrate to god.'

The pinewood workers made neck, head and legs.
Then all the parts were tenoned to each other
And treenailed fast, and shod to the wheeled stand.
Then the rough wood was polished with sea-sand
As smooth as ivory; then bronze workers
Plated the wood with bronze from battle gear
And ran fine goldwork over all the seams,
And horse-hair helmet-plumes made mane and tail.

When done, he seemed to march like a proud stallion
Bitted and decked, with an erect crest arched.

Then, when the Horse was finished, the five men
Were picked to go within: Odysseus, captain:
It was his plan; and he had been in Troy
A dozen times, dressed as a beggar, spying.
Next, Menelaus, as Queen Helen's husband,
The man with bitterest grievance against Troy.
Next, Neoptolemus, Achilles' son,
Longing to avenge his father, newly killed.
Next, Sthenelus, our best, after Achilles.
Lastly, my Father, who had made the Horse,
And claimed to share its fortunes.

                                  All these five
From gazing at the City, and from study
Of a model of the city walls and ways
Wrought by Odysseus out of river clay,
Learned all the alleys to the southern gate
That they would open... if their Fortune held.

My Father said: 'I felt like to a swimmer
Who has betted all his having on the point
That he will swim a rapid, without harm,
And then, in the cold morning, sees the torrent
That he is pledged to swim, all jagged rocks
And gliddery boulders, antlers of dead trees,
Whirlpools and waterfalls and water-snakes,
Spikes, and a rushing shriek of bloated water,
Mangling and horrid death in every yard,
And dreadful hags of water with grey arms
Tossing to pluck him to their yellow teeth;
And wishes himself far, or the deed over...

But still,' he said, 'Odysseus never doubted.'
Odysseus said: 'I answer for success
If once the Trojans bring us through the gates.'

His captaincy turned doubt into a Hope,
And what the Hope became, another tells.

from The Conway

After Forty Years

Let us walk round: the night is dark but fine,
And from the fo'c's'le we shall surely see
The lights of steamers passing to the sea,
And all the city lamp-light, line on line.

There on the flood the trampled trackways shine
With hasting gleamings shaken constantly,
The River is the thing it used to be
Unchanged, unlike those merry mates of mine.

This is the very deck, the wind that blows
Whines in the self-same rigging: surely soon
Eight bells will strike, and to his fading tune
Will come the supper-call from Wally Blair:
And then alive, from all the graves none knows,
Will come the boys we knew, the boys we were.

from The Box of Delights

[Old Rum-Chops' Song]

We fly a banner all of black,
With scarlet Skull and Boneses,
And every merchantman we take
We send to Davey Jones's.
Sing diddle-diddle-dol.

To fetch the gold out of the hold
We make them shake their shankses.
Then over the side to take a dive
We make them walk the plankses.
Sing diddle-diddle-dol.

from Victorious Troy

['When the last captives...']

When the last captives left the Skaian Gate,
And, looking back, beheld the fallen towers,
Crushing the young men's bodies in the flowers,
And heard the curses bidding them not wait,

And felt the spear-butts in the hands of hate
Strike as the stick falls on the beast that cowers,
They knew that they had done with happy hours,
Not even God could remedy their Fate.

No hope for them; but other Troys have risen,
And fallen, since, whose broken hearts have found
Comfort among the blackest nights that are,

Water in babble from the desert ground,
The Cock in carol for the Morning Star,
And Hope the living Key unlocking prison.

from A Letter from Pontus and other verse

Ballet Russe

I

The gnome from moonland plays the Chopin air,
The ballerina glides out of the wings,
Like all the Aprils of forgotten Springs.
Smiling she comes, all smile,
All grace; forget the cruel world awhile:
Forget vexation now and sorrow due.
A blue cap sits coquettish in her hair.

She is all youth, all beauty, all delight,
All that a boyhood loves and manhood needs.
What if an Empire perishes, who heeds?
Smiling she comes, her smile
Is all that may inspire, or beguile.
All that our haggard folly thinks untrue.
Upon the trouble of the moonlit strain
She moves like living mercy bringing light.

Soon, when the gnomish fingers cease to stray,
She will be gone, still smiling, to the wings,
To live among our unforgotten things,
Centaur and unicorn,
The queens in Avalon and Roland's horn,
The mystery, the magic and the dew
Of a to-morrow and a yesterday.

II

With delicate control in maddest speed
This rocket shoots and falls, and falling, twists;
Where Nature has denied, his soul insists:
Grace, strength and skill are fused.
Thus has the starry skill his matter used,
The harsh, rebellious, formless, lineless stuff
That would not soon obey, nor blend, nor heed.

This leapt above the horns of bulls in Crete;
This hunted Hector round the walls of Troy;
This brought the god into his shrine in joy;
Thus, long ago, began
Whatever beauty has begun in man,
The image being beaten from the rough,
In hungry instants by the incomplete.

February Night

I went into the land where Beauty dwells.
The winter darkness shut it as a prison.
The thin moon, due at midnight, had not risen.
The clouds moved slowly over: nothing else
Stirred, nor did owl cry, nor did glow-worm glisten.
The night in all her vastness stood to listen.
Then, in the valley church, men rang the bells.

Out of the tower into the winter air
They shook their triumph: and a hill beyond
Made laggard ghosts of echoes to respond.
As turbulent water beats the boulder bare
And hurries and leaps, so turbulent drin and drone
Clanged and were spilled in cataracts of tone
Out of the tower above the ringers there.

Then the bells ceased; the men, as I suppose
Muffling their throats in woollens, trudged to bed.
The Heaven displayed her star-work overhead
Star beyond star, the brighter as it froze.
A fox barked thrice, none answered, the world slept,
Save at some oven where a cricket kept
Trilling the drowsy cat into a doze.

Wood-Pigeons

Often the woodman scares them as he comes
Swinging his axe to split the fallen birch:
The keeper with his nim-nosed dog at search
Flushes them unaware; then the hive hums.

Then from the sheddings underneath the beech,
Where squirrels rout, the flock of pigeons goes,
Their wings like sticks in battle giving blows,
The hundred hurtling to be out of reach.

Their wings flash white above a darker fan,
In drifts the colour of the smoke they pass,
They disappear above the valley grass,
They re-appear against the woodland tan.

Now that the valley woodlands are all bare,
Their flocks drift daily thus, now up, now down,
Blue-grey against the sodden of the brown,
Grey-blue against the twig-tips, thin in air.

It is a beauty none but autumn has,
These drifts of blue-grey birds whom Nature binds
Into communities of single minds,
From early leaf-fall until Candlemas.

So in the failing Life when Death and Dread,
With axe and mongrel, stalk the withering wood,
The pigeons of the spirit's solitude
Clatter to glory at the stealthy tread,

And each, made deathless by the Spirit's joy,
Launch from the leaves that have forgotten green,
And from the valley seek another scene,
That Dread can darken not, nor Death destroy.

Autumn Ploughing

After the ranks of stubble have lain bare,
And field mice and the finches' beaks have found
The last spilled seed corn left upon the ground;
And no more swallows miracle in air;

173

When the green turf no longer hides the hare,
And dropping starling flights at evening come;
When birds, except the robin, have gone dumb,
And leaves are rustling downwards everywhere;

Then, out, with the great horses, come the ploughs,
And all day long the slow procession goes,
Darkening the stubble fields with broadening strips.

Gray sea-gulls settle after to carouse:
Harvest prepares upon the harvest's close,
Before the blackbird pecks the scarlet hips.

Partridges

Here they lie mottled to the ground unseen,
This covey linked together from the nest.
The nosing pointers put them from their rest,
The wings whirr, the guns flash and all has been.

The lucky crumple to the clod, shot clean,
The wounded drop and hurry and lie close;
The sportsmen praise the pointer and his nose,
Until he scents the hiders and is keen.

Tumbled in bag with rabbits, pigeons, hares,
The crumpled corpses have forgotten all
The covey's joys of strong or gliding flight.

But when the planet lamps the coming night,
The few survivors seek those friends of theirs;
The twilight hears and darkness hears them call.

The Towerer

Old Jarge, Hal, Walter and I, the Rector and Bill,
The old red setter and Joe, the retriever, Bess,
Went out in the cider time for something to kill,
Past Arthur's Camp, a couple of miles, I guess.

We came in the noon of the blue September day
To a tongue of grass thrust into a cleft of copse,
Berries were black and plump on the changing spray,
A dwindled spring went over its lip in drops.

We stopped to drink at the spring, Hal, Walter and I,
The retriever, Bess, the old red setter and Joe.
A covey went up with a whirr and the guns let fly,
The birds went skimming the trees towards Barney's Low.

They fired two last long shots, the Rector and Bill,
A feather came out of a bird, but the bird went on.
'Hit him,' they said; we muttered, 'You didn't kill.'
Over the tips of the trees the covey was gone.

The hit bird swerved from the line of the covey's charge,
Over the grass of the field we watched him rise:
'Got him,' the Rector said. 'Her towers,' said Jarge.
We saw him breast like a lark the hot blue skies.

He climbed the air till he struggled in sky alone,
Straining and beating up on a battling breast,
Then paused, then dropped with a thump upon bounding bone:
Joe brought him in; we bagged him up with the rest.

At covey-call time in the dusk September eve,
We loitered home together and shared the kill:
Nine brace, three rabbits, a hare: we all took leave;
Jarge took the dogs: the moon came over the hill.

Poor Bess, the retriever, died, her muzzle all white;
A run-away cart ran over the spaniel, Joe;
Jarge died of a quart of rum next Christmas night;
The old red setter went west, oh, ages ago.

Bill died from shock of a fall, as his heart was weak,
The Rector lingered to die of a sheer old age;
Walter went down with a stroke and could not speak,
He, too, has gathered his goods and drawn his wage.

Only Hal and myself of the nine remain,
And Hal's forgotten the bird, forgotten the shoot;
The grass, the wood and the spring are here in my brain,
With the dogs and the wine-leaved brambles black with fruit.

I think of the towering bird with its choking lung,
Its bursting heart, its struggle to scale the sky,
And wonder when we shall all be tried and hung
For the blue September crime when we made it die.

The Eyes

I remember a tropic dawn before turn-to,
The ship becalmed, the east in glow, a dimness,
Dark still, of fleece clouds mottled to the zenith,
The seamen as men dead upon the deck,
Save three who watched, dark statues they, dark bronze.
All things were silent save uneasy gear,
So silent that one heard the flying fish
Startling in frisk and plopping in the sea,
So many that we knew that multitudes
Of living things were near us though unseen.

Marvellously the fleece clouds changed from dim
Through every lovely colour into gold,
And then through every light to intense gleam,
Until a miracle of burning eyes
Looked down upon our thirty distinct souls.

Each of us and the fishes in the deeps,
And every flitting sprite that leapt and sped,
Those watchers knew and called each by his name.

Porto Bello

The port is unsuspected from the east,
Slowly the bay draws open, with still water,
Deeper and deeper yet, to the calm pond,
Hot, stagnant, wrinkleless, of palest gray.

There is the city at the end at last,
The dirty, gray stone platform of the fort,
To left of what remains, a few small houses,
The little river and a scarlet barn.

Once all the bells in England rang with joy
That we had captured this; we have two poems,
A painting and commemorative pots
(Jugs and quart mugs) which celebrate the feat.

Two generations since, an English ship
Lay here surveying: one aboard her told me
That all her seamen were beset with boils
Like Egypt in the Book of Exodus;
Their chart is still the sailor's guidance here.

How many English bones lie underneath
That stirless water, Drake's men; Morgan's men;
The buccaneers; all Admiral Hosier's men;
The men with Vernon; christened in the fonts
Of English churches, and now welded white
With shells, or waving scarlet with soft tendrils,
Part of a sea-floor where no anchors fall
Nor any shadow of an English ship.

Near, in the blueness of the haze, an island
Rises before us as we pass the port;
It is Escudo, where Sir Francis Drake
'Yielded his valiant spirit like a Christian.'
Some say 'His heart is buried there': perhaps.
His body lies beneath us somewhere here.
The surf breaks on the island as we pass.

A Ballad of Sir Francis Drake

Before Sir Francis put to sea,
He told his love, 'My dear,
When I am gone, you wait for me,
Though you wait for seven year.'

His love, who was redder than the rose,
And sweeter than the may,
Said, 'I will wait till summer snows
And winter fields bear hay.

I'll wait until the ice is hot,
And July sun is cold,
Until the cliffs of Dover rot,
And the cliffs of Devon mould.'

Sir Francis went aboard his ship,
Her sails were sheeted home,
The water gurgled at her lip
And whitened into foam.

And months went by, but no more word
Came from that roving soul
Than comes from the Mother Carey bird
That nests at the South Pole.

In the seventh year men gave up hope,
And swore that he was dead.
They had the bell tolled with the rope
And the burial service read.

His love, who was redder than the rose,
Mourned for him long and long,
But even grief for a lover goes
When life is running strong.

And many a man beset her way
Who thought it Paradise
To gaze at her lovely eyes and say
That her eyes were stars, not eyes.

And so she promised a nobleman
When the ninth-year hay was hauled,
And before the harvest-home began
Her marriage banns were called.

The wedding-day came bright and fair,
The bells rang up and down,
The bridesmaids in their white were there
And the parson in his gown.

The rosy bride came up the aisle,
The page-boys bore her train;
She stood by the groom a little while
To be made one out of twain.

Not one of all within the church
Thought of Sir Francis Drake.
A crash made the transept columns lurch
And the central tower quake.

A cannon-ball came thundering by
Between the bride and groom.
The girl said, 'Francis wonders why
There's someone in his room.

Francis is homing from the seas,
He has sent this message here.
I would rather be wife to Francis, please,
Than the lady of a peer.'

Ere the priest could start his talk again,
A man rushed in to say,
'Here is Drake come home with the wealth of Spain.
His ships are in the Bay.'

The noble said with courtly grace,
'It would be a wiser plan
If I let Sir Francis take my place,
And I will be Best Man.'

The Mayblossom

(Told me by the Pilot)

The ship, *Mayblossom*, left Magellan Straits
And beat into a roaring Northerly.

Slowly she thrust into the strength against her;
The screw raced, the ship trembled, the plates groaned.
Up on her bridge, her Captain and two Mates
Saw in the blindness the Evangelists,
The four great rocks forever standing guard,
All wind-shrieked, sea-swept.

Slowly she beat to westward from the rocks,
Streamed, and turned northward for her Chilean port,
A half-league, then a league, upon her course;
Then, suddenly, the ship's propeller jarred
Off from its shaft and left her helpless there.

She drifted back; the Captain called all hands.
'Men, the propeller's gone; the ship is helpless.
We shall be on the rocks within the hour.
Any of you who choose may take the boats:
I shall stay by her and go down with her.'

Half the ship's people chose to risk the boats.
One boat was smashed to pieces as she lowered.
The other, full of men, got clear away
And with a rag of sail beat from the ship
And no man ever heard of her again.
Meanwhile, the *Mayblossom*
Drifted upon the Four Evangelists;
The wind-shrieked, sea-swept.

Then, as she stumbled in the breakers' backwash,
When the great rocks hung up above the bridge,
And cataracts of billow fell back blind,
And all her fabric trembled from the blows
Of water thwarted by the basalt's face,
A wayward waif of current plucked her clear
And swept her South,
Towards the Horn,
To gray seas running forlorn,
Where ships are sown for corn,
And birds have screams in the mouth.

Having a Life and Hope and half a crew,
Captain and Engineer advised together,
Behind the dodger, as she rode the sea.
The Captain said,
'We've forty tons of gunny-sack, in bales,
Down in the forward hold: we might make sails
With that, if we had needles and some twine.
You have no twine or needles, I suppose?'
The Engineer replied, 'We used to use them;

And always, still, when I indent for stores,
I ask to have a hank of twine and needle.
There should be one of each: I'll go to see.'
Soon he came running back with shining eyes.
'Captain, a miracle has happened here:–
I wrote "One hank of twine and one sail-needle"…
(Things which I never use, one trip in ten),
But by some miracle the chandlers sent
A gross of twine and gross of sail-needles.
See here, assorted sizes, England's best.'
'You cannot beat the good God,' said the Captain,
'For when He gives, He gives beyond all hope.
Now, when we've made some palms, we'll buckle-to,
And fashion sails and pluck her out of this.'

They stitched a suit of sails: they contrived yards
From derricks, oars and handspikes: they set sail,
Ran eastward round the Horn and made the Falklands.

There, when the ship-repairers quoted terms,
The Captain told them, 'Rather than pay that,
I'll sail her to the Mainland, and try there.'

So said, so done: he sailed her to the Plate;
Shipped a propeller at a fairer price,
Then, under steam
Trudged the cold blackness of Magellan's stream
To that green water by a Chilean slip
That waited for the shadow of his ship.

Sweet Friends

Print not my life nor letters; put them by:
When I am dead let memory of me die.
Blessed be those who in their mercy heed
This heartfelt prayer of mine to Adam's Seed;
Blessed be they, but may a curse pursue
All who reject this living prayer, and do.

from The Country Scene

On England

What is this England, whom the draughtsmen print
As such and such, in ever-changing guise,
Now as a fat boor, whiskered and unwise,
Now as a shielded, trident-bearing Queen,
Now as a lion, now as a St George
Thrusting a trampled dragon through the gorge?
From what known image do they take their hint?
Where is such England met, such England seen?

England is with us where the roadway goes,
A land of downs inestimably fair,
With cornfields, apple-orchards, fruits and spires,
Night-glaring slagheaps, where men swink at fires,
Cities with chimneys blackening the air,
Ships in whatever harbour a tide flows,
A million gardens, each with lily and rose,
And football, though the grass be blasted bare.

England with mucky arms, and cheer, and spanner
Kneels at your car to help you in distress;
On many a bridge in many a crazy ship,
England in oilskins keeps a stiffened lip;
In burnt or freezing lands beyond the sea
England will welcome you to England's banner
(The chances of the football cup, and tea).
England comes nearer when the troubles press.

No man can praise her, she is full of fault;
No man can blame her, she is full of good,
Kindness, stupidity and hardihood
Wisdom and gentleness, the sweet and salt.
She grows more wise and gentle, growing old,
New stars arise, to light her to exalt
The Life within her borders above gold;
New buds are springing from the ancient wood.

To these, and to her new-crowned King and Queen,
Be blessing upon blessing, late and soon,
The hundred millions of her virtuous dead
Watch over her and guard her as she goes.
That which has been
Is past, another England lies ahead,
With beauty on her bosom as a rose
And sunrise springing at her setting moon.

Lambing

In iron midnights in the downland fold
The shepherd with a lantern tends his ewes.
The fox barks by; the midnight, tense with cold,
Stares, with her frosty eyes, at Life beginning
In skinny things, who think it unworth winning,
And one hard man who cannot let them lose.

Nomads

Where do they go, these waggons of delight,
When the last visitor has left the ground,
When all the seats are struck, and the last light
Serves but to load the tent into the van?
No herald leads the way, no trumpets sound,
The drowsy horses nudge the drowsy man,
The owls' world takes them and the nightjar sees.
The window curtains click, the wheels go round.
Declining stars behold them trudge the night.
To-morrow they will prosper and be bright,
Beauty will triumph and the clown will please.

The Gallop on the Sands

White horses toss their manes along the shore;
The horses of the sea are up and away.
We gallop in the backwash and the spray;
Sea after breaking sea
Washes the ruins of the one before.
Within our hearts we feel the horses' glee.

The Morris Dancers

Men have forgotten how the dance began.
But once, up in the wind, atop the Down,
Beyond the ditch that made the huts a town,
This fancy fired in the soul of Man:—
That, if they sacrificed with wine and bread,
And power spilled all day, in rhythm, at speed,
The god, who governs having, giving heed,
Might give again and let the tribe be fed.
That is forgotten now, but every year
The drink, the cake, the strength, are sacrificed.
All day about the street the dancers pass;
The moonrise sees them dancing on the grass;
The spirit of the Flint Age flinging here
A challenge from the æons before Christ.

The Mare and Foal at Grass

Now that the grass is at its best in May,
Before the gadfly with the jewelled eyes
Lights, on soft foot, for blood, the mare and foal
Enjoy the Sun's returning from the south,
The swallows darting and the cuckoos' toll.

The young life gallops in his holiday,
Destiny being dim and youth unwise.
Still distant are the switches on his thighs
And iron on his feet and in his mouth.

The County Show

What do they think among these staring eyes,
This crowd in tumult stopping but to stare?
They left the wonted pasture in a van
And now are here, if here be anywhere,
Amid steam organs and Aunt Sally shies,
The smell of beasts, the knaveries of man.

Strangers in cords and gaiters mock and poke,
Children climb stretching on the rails to stroke
The little trembling colt and Suffolk mare.

Elephants in the Tent

'They're not the draw they were,' the showman said.
'I never like them much; they're queer things, very.
For anything they happen on, they'll eat;
Your spanners, or goloshes off your feet:
One day you'll have em well, the next day, dead.
And take my word, they're hellish jobs to bury.'

The Roadside Inn

All passing men, with beast or waggons,
Draw in, draw up, and call for flagons,
And say it's cold, or say it's hot,
Or will be shortly, like as not;
Or say, it's time we'd sun, or rain,
Or, Mrs Jones has twins again;
Or, Rector's dead, or that girl Ann
Has gone off with a soldier man.
Or, we remember old things, we;
Or, tidden like it used to be.

Five hundred years this talk has gone
Then they have drained their mugs and paid,
And slowly watched the summer fade,
And seen the evening star and gone.

The Procession of the Bulls

Slowly, in line, the winning bulls go by,
They lurch against the air; the crowds perceive
The smoulder in the wrathful, empty eye,
The tremble in the muscle of the heave.

What memories they stir, of tribal feasts,
Of struggles in arenas, and of days
When Stone Age hunters met them as wild beasts,
Beheld those eyes, and dared not stand their gaze.

The Tight-rope Walker

The naphtha flares, the thousand faces glow,
On one bright string the tight-rope walker treads,
Or slides, or sways, or trips above our heads;
She sees such bliss, she never looks below.

What does she feel? Contempt for those who stare?
Or simple joy, that after years of care
This miracle of balance comes like breath?
Or peace, that she is daily risking Death
For daily bread, nor fears him anywhere?

Their Canvas Home

This is the Circus tent, where the tribe camps
For some brief hours while they give the show.
The tethered piebalds whicker in their row;
At little fires little groups make tea.
Artists and clowns and ponies come and go,
And at his iron pickets restlessly
An elephant rocks sideways, broods and stamps.
This is the hunting-ground until the boys
Slacken the canvas and unship the pole;
Then, one by one, the lamp-lit waggons start
By summer-drowsy lanes where the moth dreams.
Forth fare they, to new conquests of the soul,
Forth, to new laughers at the ancient part,
Another pitch, the sawdust and the noise.

The Horse and Trap at the Ford

Three thousand years ago this track was used
Across and through this water; every day
In all that living, this has been the way,
By hoof and foot-tread have the stones been bruised.

Under the water wimpling from the wheels
What relics lie of fairings dropped and drowned,
The precious pennies, sought, but never found,
The calkin scattered from the punches' heels.

Fragments of food, dropped as the horses drank,
Flint arrow-heads worn smooth, old chains from waggons,
Sherds of red Samian ware, the lips of flagons,
And links once bright upon a Viking's flank.

The Horse in the Barn

Into this barn these horses have dragged corn
Each Summer, for five hundred anxious years.
Full many a hundred horse-shoes have been worn
To bright, thin streaks upon the ash-pit hurled
In homing harvest safe amidst these piers;
The old horse in the old barn stands forlorn,
The war-horse of the war that saves the world.

The Ploughing Match

This is the work that keeps the world alive;
Vanity, wisdom, pomp and misery
Alike are nourished by these straining teams;
The plough-share turns the red wave of a sea;
With clink and creak of harness up they strive,
The lark flits, the man steadies, the roots rive,
The grave eyes peer beneath a brow that streams.

It is the noblest labour done by men,
Here are its champions with their noble slaves;
With whatsoever madness the world raves
Doing as these it might be wise agen.

Hunting

Ah, once, in the world's youth, men crept like snakes
Along the grass, or glid from tree to tree,
Or petrified to immobility
At any twig-fall in the forest-brakes;
Then crept again, or waited, hour by hour,
The silent-footed prey with wrinkling nose,
Those unheard darknesses, the stag and does.

Ah, then, either the bowman tasted power,
His arrow riving in the knocking heart,
Or disappearing hooves flung leaves askart,
And meatless tribesmen mourned the fool's mistakes;

Now all is idle, but the idlest still
Feels in his marrow the ancestral thrill.

The old King in the barrow on the brae,
Spoke to his hounds thus, when the world was young,
Thus tense, the knights on Ida, centuries since,
Harked to the horn of Priamus the prince;
Thus Meleager viewed the boar away,
And man's heart leaped with hound's heart and gave tongue.

Timber Hauling

Once, he was undergrowth which the stag spared,
The stag, and the wild bull, and the wild horse,
His rootings sucked the Earth's milk into force;
Up, past his enemies, he thrust and flared.
Then, looking out, he saw the Heavens bared,
The Sun, the Moon, the many-lighted sky;
The raincloud caught his boughs in blowing by;
His thickets sheltered every bird that paired.

In his green triumph he surveyed the grass
With men who faded like it; he beheld
Monarch on monarch of his forest felled;
He saw three hundred cuckoo-comings pass.

Then axe-heads rived him from his pride of place;
With a slow, stripping crash his kingship downed.
Starlings at twilight seek another roost.
Jaggings of splinter stab the trampled ground.
Sunlight revisits patches long unused
All chittered with the marks of his disgrace.

The Gipsies in the Snow

The bitter evening falls, the fog's about,
The horses droop and steam, the fire fails,
The gipsies huddle, blowing on their nails,
The Cold, the Enemy of Life, assails,
Life, the humped bison, bows, to keep him out.

from Tribute to Ballet

The Foreign Dancers

After the cuckoo's coming thrills the valley
With cry long longed-for, long unheard, the plumtrees
Are white as brides with blossom; then the apples
Bud red and white upon the harsh boughs silver;
Then swallows come again to their mud pouches.
Then all is Spring, and you, the dancers, gather,
West, with the Spring, the papers tell your coming.
Beauty and Joy have come again to London.

But what is London to yourselves but somewhere
To dance in nightly for a ballet-season;
A theatre with call-boys, draughty stairways,
Music, a great crowd hushed, late-comers stumbling,
Then shirt-fronts, staring eyeballs, and hands clapping,
Until the curtain falls upon the climax,
Then men in uniform with gifts of roses,
Then midnight streets and lamplight to the lodging?

But what are you to us, O radiant dancers?
After the winter of our prose and sickness,
The bones of old belief and news of murder,
You bring together all that makes men happy,
Colour and lovely movement and sweet music,
Old fable breathed upon to make new beauty,
The grace and elegance of gentle women,
The power and the courtesy of knighthood.

O you are roses of too swift a Summer.
Too soon, too soon, the curtain falls in flowers,
I see your well-loved faces at the footlights,
Bowing farewell; since nightingales have left us,
You, too, must off into some world of strangers.
While we, without you, cannot pass the portals
Within which you have danced, without a quiet,
The ghost of some great joy that you have given.

Though there be little need to tell your wonder
(Your dancing tells it, all the world confirms it),
The giving thanks is sweet. You do not know me.
I am but one among your crowd of starers,
One of the blur of shirt-fronts and hands clapping.
Instead of sending flowers at the curtain,
I offer you these words of thanks and praises,
The dumbness of a some one who is no one.

Long hence, perhaps, when I am in the downland,
Under the larks' nests and the small blue milkworts,
You, aged men and women, by the fire,
Seeing, perhaps, your great grand-children, dancing,
May think, 'Ah, once, when I was young as you are,
I danced as you dance, and was famous for it;
A poet praised my dancing in his verses,'
And read again these lines, long since forgotten.

The Indian Dancers

I watched the quiet, age-old Indian art;
They danced the harvest-dance, in which a boy,
Filled by an evil spirit, falls and dies.
There was an end of all the simple joy
Attending on the reaping of the rice.
For no child dies but leaves a broken heart.

Then from the wings a wizard figure crept,
Strange, bent, forbidding, with a muffled head,
A crone more like to murder than to heal.
She bent above the body of the dead;
I watched her crooked doctor-fingers feel.
This I had seen from childhood; my heart leapt.

For this was but the Christmas Mummers' play.
This was but Mrs Vinney at the corpse
Dealing the famous pill that routed Death;
And I remembered nights in English thorpes,
The lantern-light, the snow upon the way,
Crunching to hob-nailed boots, the frosted breath,

The six good men and true in paper-strips,
All blue and pink and dripping as they went
Wielding their wooden swords to act again
The Turk and great St George in tournament;
And battering the passers in the lane
With bladders on the lashes of their whips.

Most strange it was to see the ancient root
From which the Mummers sprang; oh, by what ways,
Over the mountains and the burning sands
And thrustings back and century delays,
And wanderings in green or snowy lands,
Had come the seeds or graftings of such fruit?

There was the stock, inscrutable and strange,
Of men, remote from life, who keep apart
In the clear light to meditate on Man.
Undying are the impulses of art,
In living thought it dwells as it began,
Hope, the Almighty, overcoming Change.

The Class

It is the break; the pupils are at rest,
They sketch the arabesques they cannot dare
And give each other hints, with mock and jest.

The famous Master watches from his chair,
He is a little man with robin's eyes,
His choicest pupil sits beside him there.

To-day, she is the Ballet's brightest star;
They joke together with their memories.
The pupils watch her, backed against the barre.

The fiddler sucks a sweet and cons a score,
His damp, thin hairs about his temples cling.
The Mistress fills the can and starts to pour.

She is a little woman, dusky-faced,
All wire, whipcord, whalebone and steel spring,
For every effort exquisitely braced.

Now that the floor is watered, she commands
The steps to follow, which her feet display.
Swift, the last slipper rubs among the sands,

Tensely, the dancers wait upon the beat.
It falls, the music sounds; away, away,
Drumlike the running batter of the feet

Tramples until the flooring seems to sway,
Swiftly she urges them with voice and hands,
They ripple like the wind upon the wheat.

Up, down and sideways go the flying feet,
No step escapes the watchers as they dance.
All Russia is on honour with all France.

The bud, the promise, and the incomplete...
Which will emerge? For surely one or more,
When this, the budding is a rose of May,
And that, the April, is a summer day,
Will snatch the golden star from flying chance
And hear the world's praise rising to a roar.

Rehearsal

Green rollers shatter into hands that shoot
And clutch, and fail, and fall; and others follow.
The sun burns in blue Heaven, the bees hum,
A lizard glistens on the fig tree root.
Leave now, the sunlight, for this tunnel's hollow...
This is the Tower, here is Roland come.

Imagine a vast room, unwindowed, lit
By bulbs on cables stretched across the ceiling.
One wall is looking-glass, the rest are white,
With dancers' barres and sand-box full of grit.
The floor is laid with narrow yellow dealing.
Here are the preparations of delight.

There are no furnishings, save chairs that fold
Close to the wall, and this piano propping
A score, bound in blue paper, of Mozart.
But now the shepherd calls his flock to fold,
Forth, from within, the company comes hopping,
And groups are posed before rehearsals start.

Most of the dancers wear black practice-dress,
With coloured kerchiefs on their temples banded,
Pale shoe-straps cross their ankles; most are young;
With chatter and with laughter and caress
They sit or lie in grouping as commanded,
The women's scarves upon the barres are hung.

Twenty or thirty others gather; some
Are famous through the planet for their graces.
Keenly they watch the posing of the groups.
Their chaff and chatter makes a merry hum.
The regisseur with pencil plots the places,
The posers rise and join the other troupes.

Now the producer calls, and at the call
Beginners hurry; the piano, playing
That long-familiar Mozart, starts the play.
Like tappings upon drums the footings fall.
Imagined passion sets the puppets swaying...
The Master claps his hands, the dancers stay.

He speaks reproof, corrects a pose, improves
What had seemed ragged, then, again the story
Swings to the music, and the tale unfolds.
Now like a race-course under racers' hooves
The planking quakes, the music brings a glory.
Then the hands clap, the tune stops, the voice scolds.

Meanwhile, beside a dusty crate of props,
A famous dancer poses at the glasses
Correcting movements of the arms and hands.
He seeks a beauty never sold in shops,
He seeks the star that lightens and surpasses,
The deathless star, when what is mortal stops,
And spirit poises timeless without bands.

The Seventh Hungarian Dance of Brahms

Underneath the curtains edged with moth-gnawn gold
Stood a splintry staging dark with unscrubbed mould.
The footlights lit not, the piano had a cold,
The seven rows of stalls were empty.

Then upon the music came the footfall light,
You had brought the sunshine to the death-vault's blight,
Brought the spring and sunshine and the year's delight
And all the birds of April singing.

Masks

Often, the books about the ancients told
That actors had used masks, but never how.
'Masks were an adjunct of the past,' we thought,
'A savagery, for savage dances wrought,
Adapted to the theatres of old,
Then cast aside, and well-forgotten now.'

Then, suddenly, we saw them made alive,
Tragic or comic at a dancer's will,
And, as Ulysses saw the spirits drive
Numberless, piteous, proud, we were aware
Of all a great past's passion standing there
And all man's living spirit quaking still.

Where They Took Train

Gomorrah paid so for its holiday;
The east wind bit the ears and snapped the skin,
Snow-pellets made the meadow-ridges gray,
The sky was like a punishment for sin.

Then the old cage-like bus, from this old inn,
Gathered you birds of beauty as its prey,
And like a morgue the station took you in,
And like a hearse the train bore you away.

Bore you away, to sad and happy Fate;
All up and down the world your feet have gone,
Some, to much glory, not yet all fulfilled.
Now, in that dingy station as I wait,
I think, 'Among these stones their beauty shone,'
Then I forget the present and am thrilled.

The Painter of the Scene

Twenty years since, your pale, distinguished face,
Full of despair, the face of one heart-broken,
Was turned to mine; we muttered and shook hands.

Contact of twenty seconds in two lives.

If I had known, that after twenty years,
My heart would ache to have again those seconds,
To thank you for the marvel of your gift,
Might I have changed that look still haunting me?

Not Only The Most Famous

No, for their names are written with the light
Over the roof, and they are ever praised,
Called and recalled for flowers every night,
And daily lunched and laurelled by the crazed.

Let them enjoy their glory; it is earned;
But, for myself, I love the two or three
For whom no sign upon the roof has blazed,
No lilies on the curtain-fall been white;
In whom, unthanked, the unfed flame has burned,
The snowdrop beauty that the lonely see.

from Some Memories of W.B. Yeats

On His Tobacco Jar

This is the dull red jar of earthenware
Which held Virginian cigarettes on Mondays;
The embossed decoration of black dragons
Is now much worn away; the side is pitted;
The knobbed lid has been cracked and rivetted;
Thirty years past I bargained with him for it.
What hands have dipped for cigarettes within you;
What Monday companies have looked upon you:
The writers and the painters and the speakers,
The occultists, the visionary women,
Astrologers with Saturn on their moons,
And contemplative men who lived on herbs
And uttered gentleness and sanctity,
The poets of the half-a-dozen schools,
Young men in cloaks, velvet, or evening dress;
Publishers, publicists and journalists,
Parliament men, who served the Irish cause,
And every Irish writer, painter and thinker.

This dull red earthen jar was on his table
When Lady Gregory took up the script
And read Synge's earliest plays to the small group.
It stood amidst our pleasure and Synge's pride.
It stood among the first experiments
Of speaking poetry to notes of music,
When Florence Farr, who died a Buddhist nun,
Took up the psaltery which Dolmetsch made
And spoke Ulysses taking up the bow
Or sang about the lover and his lass.
What wisdom, merriment and various beauty
Have played about this clay, and what gay scenes.
Blithe Pixie, singing Yeats's songs or telling
West Indian tales with her bright painted dolls.
And that kind visionary man who saw
The long-past lives of each of us in turn
And always rightly taking from each one
Some constant thought, image, recurring dream,
Which was, he said, the lingering memory
Kept by the self of its passed pilgrimage.

Outside, the shadows of the plane-trees danced
Amid the lamplight; the blind beggar shifted
From foot to foot; the little children screamed
At the road junction at the Buildings' end;
And night-men seeking after drinks and drabs
Moved towards pots and shawls under the lamps.
Yet in that upper room round the red jar
Each one of us was touched to a romance
Believing in that image of the past.
There was a strangeness and a poetry
About that place; the blind man by the lamp
By day, was a tea-taster in the City.
Within the gloomy churchyard at our backs
Godwin and Mary Wollstonecraft had lain.
There, the young Thomas Hardy years before
Had helped to lift a coffin which broke open
Displaying a man's bones and two men's skulls.

There one among us told how he had gone
To see a visionary Russian woman,
Within whose presence exquisite bright flowers
Fell from the ceiling; he had gathered these
And borne them home, and all who met him saw
And praised their beauty and their scent; alas
No trace remained of them when morning came.

Perhaps no-one of us within the room
But felt that any beauty might begin
At any moment there, that some red cock
Would perch upon the settle and cry Morning,
That then the ceiling and the walls would fade
And blue anemones be at our feet,
And horses with red ears come whinnying fast,
To bear us thence, to islands of desire
Where the never-dying Phoenix sings in fire,
Where the givers, and the wise ones and the wonders
Dispense their shining bread amid their peace.

['Willy's Geese...']

Somebody said, 'All Willy's geese are swans
To Willy:'
                        true; and lucky for the geese.
He 'always encouraged everybody; always.'

No man in all this time has given more hope
Or set alight such energy in souls.
There was no rush-wick in an earthen saucer
Half-filled with tallow, but he made it burn
With something of a light for somebody.

from The Nine Days Wonder

Thoughts for Later On

When someone somewhere bids the bombing cease,
And ships unharassed ply at Life's demands,
And friends again greet friends in foreign lands,
And sad survivors call the ruin peace,

Then, peace will be but ruin, unless Thought
Of how the peace was purchased be in mind,
Of how, to buy it, men are lying blind
Under the sea in ruined wreckage caught;

Thinking of them, and those who rode the air,
Or shogged the Flanders plain in Belgium's aid,
Or stood at Cassel with the grand Brigade,
Peace may be filled with beauty everywhere,

If, with each purchased breath, we vow to give
To Earth the joy they never lived to live.

Not any drums nor bugles with Last Post
For these men dead in intellect's despite.
Think not of war as pageant but as blight
Famine and blasting to the pilgrim ghost.

So, for the brave men fallen for man's crime
The young men beautiful all unfulfilled,
The broken and the mangled and the killed.
For whom no Spring can come in cuckoo-time

Let there be beauty spilt like holy seed
Not any mock of custom or parade
But hope atoning for the ruin made
And shame alike for deed and want of deed.

from A Generation Risen

The Paddington Statue

Twenty-five years ago, another crowd
Of seamen, airmen, soldiers, mustered here
Their caps beneath the kitbags sideways bowed,
Full many a thousand taking train to death.
As dark, as fatal is the present year
As gay a youth still draws as threatened breath.

Above them, in his bronze, their forebear stands
The lonely unknown warrior of the race
(Careless of plumes and military bands,
And eminents whom nothing ever teaches),
Who stands unhelped in many deadly breaches
And at long last puts despots in their place.

The Station

Dingy, unpainted, dark, war and November,
Paddington Station, dusk, before the black-out,
Wreathings of smokings curling, smoke-smell, fog-smell,
Number One Platform.

Once, on a Friday, here, Jamaican ship-trains,
Negroes with scarlet turbans and green parrots,
Creoles with soft-gold ear-rings, fans, mantillas,
Much Spanish spoken.

To-night, a troop-train, every window crowded
With soldiers' heads, the racks postal with kitbags,
A canteen offering tea; forward, men singing,
Aft, cheers and catcalls.

There, to a side, a lad and lover parting,
He, in greatcoat, with pack, rifle and gasmask,
She, in her very best, to shew the regiment
Her love's discernment.

They kiss, with broken hearts, they part, he shoulders
With one great heave, his load of gear, his sorrow,
His destiny, the world that Time's abortions
Bring the true-hearted.

Paddington. Mother and Son

He sees his comrades, and a coming test
In which he hopes to shine, not yet perceiving
How mud may soil a fallen Hector's crest,
And Priam's palace echo with girls grieving.

She only sees her son, her life's one star,
The leaping little lad of days that were,
Somewhere alone amid the wreck of war,
Crying for help from her and she not there.

Two Soldiers Waiting

They lived in the same town, but never met
Until the war, when Fate her cursed yoke
Of equal suffering on Europe set.
Now, from a common impetus to bear,
Has sprung the sympathy to give and share,
To count the silly Colonel as a joke
And try to tame the sergeant as a pet.

Sentries

Throughout the night, they stare into the dark
For what in any darkness may be here,
As silently as any snake or shark
As deadly as the Sister with the shear.
Alert, in eye and ear,
They judge the ripple and the fox's bark.

They wonder if the mist now wreathing-in,
Be filled with shapes as silent and as grey
Or what, beyond there, made the dogs begin,
And why the water splashed so, in the bay,
What death's essay
Made that unseen hare scurry on the whin.

They watch, they wonder, as in other years
In other wars, men stared into the night
For step or whisper of the men with spears
Or padding of the wolf before the light,
The east grows white.
Another night is over with its fears.

Crews Coming Down Gangways

After long watching of the fatal sea,
And anxious peering at the deadly air,
The peril ends, the mariners are free,
They step with baggage down the narrow stair.

There is no danger seamen have not run:–
Tempests have drowned them since the world began,
They have dared shipwreck, frostbite and the sun,
But these have dared a greater horror: Man.

from On the Hill

Blown Hilcote Manor

In perfect June we reached the house to let,
In remote woodland, up a private lane,
Beyond a pond that seemed as black as jet
Whereon a moorhen oared with chickens twain;
And from the first a sense of want or debt
Seemed to possess the place from ancient pain.

Then, turning Right, we had the House in view,
A red Victorian brick – with earlier stone,
Fair, but unhappy, being overgrown
With all the greenness Summer ever grew.
Above, about, the Summer sky was blue,
And drowsy doves intoned their purrilone.

But though abundant Summer shed her grace,
A look sufficed, to tell a wanderer there
That Death and Sorrow of Soul had hurt the place,
Stricken its life and plucked its glory bare.
No tick of time, no bell-chime, charmed the air;
The clock had stopped; we saw an empty case.

The House was dead, with doors and windows shut.
No chimney smoked; no broom, no bucket, plied;
Under the pampas at the border-side
A humping rabbit shewed a flash of scut.
How many Summers since the lawn was cut?
I plucked the door-bell's pull; no bell replied.

Then, as I sought another door, a sense
Startled my mind, a sense my comrade shared,
That all the House was glad, because suspense
(Long there) was finished, and a peace declared.
Blank on the uncut grass the windows stared,
But, oh, delighted souls were gazing thence.

A tall French-window in a garden room
Was latchless and ajar; we entered in.
The place seemed full of folk, expecting whom?
A Household mustered there, expecting kin…
Someone most dear, perhaps estranged by sin,
Or lacking absolution from the tomb.

Through open doors we looked into rooms bare
All, sensibly inhabited with glee,
And happy folk seemed coming down the stair
From sunny bedrooms in eternity,
Although we might not talk with them nor see
We felt the joy they wanted us to share.

The Manor brimmed with happiness unknown
From sorrows ending and beloved return.
Death having perished, hell was overthrown,
And spirits there made festal fires burn,
And ours, too, for, did we not discern
Love, living on, not dying all alone?

Men in their misery forever pray
For any gleam, for any certain ray,
From light beyond the mirk they struggle through.
This certainty of living love we knew
At Hilcote Manor, off the Icknield Way,
On Monday, June the sixth, in 'thirty two.

The Wind of the Sea

Three sailor-men from Bantry Bay
Ventured to sea on Christmas Day
It blows.
The wind of the sea torments us.

Out in the sea one found his grave
Although the others strove to save.
They strove as hard as men can do
But only saved their shipmate's shoe;
His shoe, his hat, his wooden fid,
And tinder-box with painted lid.
It blows.
The wind of the sea torments us.

His weeping Mother went to pray
At St Anne's Church on Bantry Bay.
She prayed like many another one,
'O sweet Saint, give me back my Son.'
Swiftly St Anne made answer wise:–
'He waits for you in Paradise.'
The Mother laughed and went her way
Back to her home and died that day.
It blows.
The wind of the sea torments us.

from The Bluebells and other verse

A Cry to Music

Speak to us, Music, for the discord jars;
The world's unwisdom brings or threatens Death.
Speak, and redeem this misery of breath
With that which keeps the stars
Each to her point in the eternal wheel
That all clear skies reveal.

Speak to us; lift the nightmare from us; sing.
The screams of chaos make the daylight mad.
Where are the dew-drenched mornings that we had
When the lithe lark took wing?
Where the still summers, when more golden time
Spoke to us, from the lime?

Though these be gone, yet, still, Thy various voice
May help assuage the pangs of our distress,
May hush the yelling where the fiends rejoice,
Quiet the sleepless, making sorrow less.
Speak, therefore, Music; speak.
Calm our despair; bring courage to the weak.

Ah, lovely Friend, bring wisdom to the strong,
Before a senseless strength has all destroyed.
Be sunlight on the night of brooding wrong.
Be form upon the chaos of the void.
Be Music; be Thyself; a prompting given
Of Peace, of Beauty waiting, and sin shriven.

The Strange Case of Captain Barnaby

There seems to be no doubt that, in or about the year 1687, a Mrs Booty,
the widow of a brewer, caused the trial of Captain Barnaby in the Court
of King's Bench, 'in a Suit of £1,000 damages', for the defamation of her
late husband's character, by the repetition of the tale told here.

The case was heard before the Chief Justice, Herbert, and three Judges,
Wythens, Holloway and Wright.

Members of the crews of three small ships swore that they had seen Mr
Booty driven into a fiery furnace on the island of Stromboli at 3.14p.m.
on the previous 15 May, as they rested ashore there, after killing curlews
for sea-store.

The Chief Justice declared that such testimony could not be doubted,
and that they had seen Mr Booty, however strange and awful the tale might
seem: Mrs Booty therefore lost her case.

We were bound home, when, on the second day
We raised the Fiery island and drew near.
We marked one glowing cranny smoking gray,
But all else glittered green and promised cheer.
The brooks were sparkling, and the birds in air
Uncountable as snow-flakes and as lovely.

So, being short of water and of meat,
I bade my consorts anchor, and then land.
We filled the barrels of our little fleet,
Then in a long line forming, gun in hand,
We walked the grass and shot the grey sea-geese,
The great St Martin's plovers and sea-curlews.

Enough, for all three ships, to last us in.
At the grass-edge, I bade the shooting cease.
But then we saw a most strange game begin.
Prone in the grass we watched it at our ease.
A negro and a white seemed playing tag
Down on the sea-beach where the boats were lying.

I cannot call to mind who saw them first,
But some one called 'Who are they? None of ours.'
As all men know, the island is accurst,
Unvisited except in daylight hours.
No other ship than ours rode the bay,
Yet here two strangers played at Snap and Dodger.

We were two hundred yards at least away.
Our keepers of the boats were watching, too.
The couple dodged the east side of the bay.
And one thing in the game we swiftly knew:
The black was bent on driving him to us,
The white one tried to pass him and get eastward.

Now we, to westward, lay below the scree
Above which, in the rock, the cranny glowed
Red, sometimes, putting colour on the sea,
Then dimming into dusk as the fumes flowed.
We heard our boatmen hail them: no reply
Came from the two intent upon their dodging.

The next thing that we noticed was the speed,
The unusual speed, with which the negro ran,
Not only swift, but tireless, indeed
A leopard or a greyhound of a man,
And every burst or effort to get by
Was headed back, towards us, nearer, nearer.

Mostly, the white man's face was to the east;
We saw the black face better, clear-cut, lean,
Something betwixt an Arab and a priest
With every faculty intently keen.
He wore black runners' shorts, close to the skin
And never wild-cat watched his quarry better.

And then, we marvelled that the dodgers paid
No heed whatever to us twenty men
Prone on the grass, watching the game they played:
We were as accidents beyond their ken,
They were intent upon an unknown game
On which (we felt assured) big stakes depended.

Then, as they neared, the white man's figure seemed
Familiar, somehow, to me, shape and pose
Perhaps some recollection of dream dreamed.
Then suddenly (by this time they were close)
I saw his face, and cried 'For the sea's sake
Why… this is Mr B, my next-door neighbour.'

Then both my mates, and others of my crew
Agreed 'Old Mr B, marine-purveyor,'
A not too honest one, as well we knew
For many a horse-shoe lay in many a layer
Of skin and bone purveyed by him as beef.
We hailed him: 'Mr B…' he took no notice.

None, but he turned, not seeing us, not knowing,
Only exhausted, and the black one sprang
Gripped him and carried to the cranny glowing,
Which opened red and took them with a clang,
One instant they glowed red, then the rocks clashed;
The smoke blew clear: the rock face bore no cranny.

Then, truly, we were on our feet, aghast.
What had we seen but someone borne to hell
Dragged to the doom of flames that ever last
One whom we all had seen and some knew well.
The cranny had closed-to upon the pair
A little smoke curled upward from the rock-face.

We crept toward the rock, hot to the feet,
Plainly appalling heat was just within…
And growlings of great powers shook the heat;
We were at Hell, the punishment of sin.
White-faced, without a word we took our loads
Back to the boats, and so aboard, for England.

So, reaching home, I asked for Mr B.
Friends, he had died that very hour and day
When we had watched him hunted by the sea
Into Hell's door a thousand miles away.
Died in distress, they said, for things ill done.
Had what we seen been his eternal sentence?

Well… our tale spread, that we had seen him borne
Into Hell fire by a thing of Hell,
And Mrs B. soon heard, you may be sworn.
As you suppose, she did not take it well.
She heard a Captain's wife repeat the tale
And sued her, straight, for slandering her husband.

Perhaps the Captain's Wife had touched the tale:
I know not, but the widow's case was brought
With all hands summoned and forbid to sail
And nothing talked of more and little thought.
Till there we were a-kissing Books in court
Before Lord Justice and the other Judges.

Mind, thirty-five of us had seen the pair,
Those in the ships, those in the boats, and we
And each one of these twenty last could swear
That beyond doubt the white was Mr B…
His hair, his venerable look, his eyes…
A mark, where a dog bit him, on his knuckles.

So, having heard, the Lord Chief Justice spoke.
'No stranger case has ever yet been tried.
What seemed at first an ill-intentioned joke
Stands, now, unique, no precedent to guide:
You have heard twenty men confirm the fact.
This was no fiction, but a witnessed act.

However strange, however out of reason,
Beyond all doubt, they tell of what they saw,
A thing most terrible, a granted sight
Of Justice done by an eternal law
That without statute ministers the right.
This the condemning Justice let them see
For purpose not revealed, but surely righteous.

The case before us fails.'
                                    So the Court cleared,
And we, no longer held, at once set sail
We ran the colours up with guns and cheered.
With ebb to help us and a topsail gale
By midnight we could see the lights of France,
By cockcrow we were running past the Foreland.

from Old Raiger and other verse

Jane

In June time once, as I was going
Up Happen Hill, by Lobs's Pound,
I saw THEM, many as snow snowing,
Hymning their Queen and dancing round.

In glitter and sparkle they were turning,
Scattering dewdrops in the green,
Their jewels shone, their eyes were burning,
And O the Beauty of their Queen.

And O the beauty of their singing,
It was as beautiful as She,
Perfect in tune, in time, and bringing
A deathlessness to mortal me.

So Life, I knew, has this for kernel,
This marvel, to which man is blind:
We make a blur round an Eternal
For ever shaming humankind.

They streamed away, away, before me,
With chimes like little silver bells,
They opened doors of glory for me,
And now I think of nothing else.

Pawn to Bishop's Five

I stayed, once, at Tom's house, at Uppats Lea,
In a green valley, where a brook rejoiced,
The happiest place wherein a boy could be,
In the first sun, in April, many-voiced.
I had played chess with Tom out of a book,
In which a master, in a champion's game,
Played Pawn to Bishop's Five, and overcame...
And all the great attack was clear to me.

Tom had some other task, I was alone,
I wandered to the brook, seeing the board
With all the pieces into vision grown,
Making the seven moves till Mate was scored.
Pawn, zig-zag Knight, sectarian Bishop, Rook,
Alive in me, and well-remembered yet.
Youth may attain what age cannot forget...
I crossed the brook, hopping from stone to stone.

And being, then, in wood, went up the stream
That ran in shade, wide, shallow, brightly-falling
On many stones, with many a sunny gleam,
And ever hurrying on, and ever calling.
Lush, brittle alder sprays and bramble-thorn
Checked my adventure, but I held my course,
Saying, 'I'll trace this water to its source.'
The chess-game filled my mind like a glad dream.

Most certainly, the wildness of the place
Showed that few people ever trod that wood.
Of pathway and of footprint were no trace,
The babbling water spoke to solitude.
With face and fingers scratched, and jacket torn,
I came out into moorland green and lone
Where the brook's being lipped over a stone,
Giving the spot an ecstasy of grace.

Though this was near, I somehow feared to tread
The slope to see from whence the water spilled.
Explorer's triumph overcame the dread...
I saw a shallow hollow, nearly filled
With water, trembling up from a stone floor.
And there, intently, in the April sun,
In water, among water-weed, was one,
Nay, two, playing with chessmen, white and red.

Spring's very self gave beauty to the pool;
A wild white cherry let her petals drip
Into the clearness, to go sailing cool
In wrinkling water, to the stony lip.
All April's gayest gems the selvage wore;
Primroses, violets, both white and blue,
Daisies, the best that ever fed on dew,
With all May's oxlips and her lady-smocks.

But O, the Indian Prince who played the chess:
The Spirit of the Brook, clear-eyed and proud,
Playing the Red men with a Chieftainess
Who played the White, over the water bowed,
The chessboard on a grassy stone between.
The Spirit of the Brook lounged half-submerged,
His latest move an utter crisis urged,
She, whom he played with, seemed oppressed and cowed.

Sure of his game, he waited, overbold,
Insolent, smiling, mocking her who played,
Yet having grace that never could grow old,
Lounged in the swaying cress his body swayed.
She turned as I approached: she was a Queen,
Queen of the violets, for blue and white
Violets made her raiment all delight.
He could not die, and she could never fade.

They saw me as not seeing, so I neared.
I was not terrified, but stricken dumb...
These were the fairies that so many feared,
And so few saw, myself the lucky some.
I crept nearer to see, perhaps to pray
To those small marvels so intensely live...
Was theirs the beauty to which souls arrive:
Perfected spirits, who have overcome?

And, staring down, I saw upon the board
The very game that so delighted me
Before the pawn's advancement drew the sword
And led the White attack to victory.
Though, still, the Princess doubted what to play,
She pondered, while her face, clear with bright thought,
In depth of wonder and of beauty wrought
As a young child's will, looking at the sea.

Yet, still, she wondered, while the Indian Prince
Mocked her delay, thinking the battle won:
His look I have remembered ever since,
While her dear spirit mustered, one by one,
The moves to turn the game a happier way.
And all my being burned into intense
Dear love for her, to quell his insolence
And snap his self-conceited malison.

And, knowing all the game from that same pause,
The move that loosed White pieces to success
In swift and certain ruin of Red's cause,
My spirit burned the clue to the Princess:
'The Pawn to Bishop's Five'; the words so clear,
And the succeeding moves so fiery bright
They danced there, like a little stream of light,
Thought being light in all her higher laws.

'The Pawn to Bishop's Five'… and lo, she heard:
Or knew, and saw, and for an instant gazed
With thanks into my face without a word.
The beauty of her thanking left me dazed,
It was so sweet, so exquisitely dear,
Herself so beautiful past power to tell.
She played the pawn at once, and the blow fell.
The mocker with the Red men ceased to gird.

His dark face blenched with fury, his hand crushed
A captured Bishop into coral grits,
And flung them where the current strongly gushed;
Like little scarlet raindrops fell the bits.
He said: 'You mate in seven moves: it's clear…
These mortals who come treading everywhere…
Let them, in future, tremble and beware
Of tempest in their blood, storm in their wits.'

He beat his hand upon the board, that broke;
The pieces vanished, he himself was gone,
The princess faded like a tiny smoke.
The water trembled up and eddied on,
Over the wet lip of the little weir.
No trace of chess or players, sound or sight,
Stayed in that water-garden of delight:
The weeds swayed, the brook babbled, the sun shone.

And I, much moved, returned another way,
And never told a soul what I had seen;
But marked the day as a red-letter day;
Had not my prompting helped a fairy queen?
Sometimes in certain spots I felt her near,
Thanking me once again with that shy look.
I kept away thenceforward from the brook.
The promised storm and tempest have not been.

Lines for the Race of Sailing Ships, Lisbon to the Hudson Bridge, near Manhattan, 1964

Once, they were Queens, triumphant everywhere,
In every port their countless house-flags flew;
Wherever wind blew billows they were there
Smashing their shadows as they thrusted through.
All the world's commerce was their occupation,
Men cheered them going forth and entering in,
Each venture showed another crown to win.

I, who beheld them in their pride of old,
Cannot forget their splendour as they came
Superb, out of the perils never told,
Hoisting their colours and the four-flag name,
And the cable-rattle of their exultation
As anchor fell ere anchor-watch was set;
Who that beheld such vision can forget?

Today, the few survivors show again
Their glory of man's triumph over force;
Over the tumult of the seas they strain
Against the westers battling out the course,
The world's great sailing ships in emulation,
Their seamen praying to be first to hail
A New York pilot-schooner under sail...

Soon they will reach into the wondrous Bay,
The harbour, Mannahatta, the world's pride;
There, be the racer's fortune what it may,
Glory and grace attend on every side;
The flags of the great ships of every nation;
The towering City shining in the sun;
And the dear quiet after effort done.

There, each in place, the contestants will moor
Beneath the Statue lightening the world...
Masters and mates and men will make all sure,
All square the mighty yards, all canvas furled.
Then, with three cheers, the seamen each in station
Will haul the colours down and hoist the lights
And beating bells begin the festal rites.

King Gaspar and His Dream

I had not meant to utter to men's ears
The holy things from which my spirit bleeds,
But I have done with sorrow, and Death nears,
And (being old) none cares (if any heeds).
But in a dream the glory that was She
Shone in my spirit and enlightened me.

This was my dream: there was a monstrous sky
Thund'rous with storm before me as I stood,
And two gray granite towers, four-square, high,
Were right and left, unutterably good.
Upon their roofs were pyramids untold
Of Paradise's fruits all glowing gold.

The doors and windows of the towers were fast,
Shuttered and barred, no person went or came,
But brightness smote those towers like a blast
And lit the empurpled darkness with its flame:
So may a winter sunsetting illume
A pine wood upon downland from its gloom.

And She was there, illuminously bright
Clad as in sky, so jewel-studded o'er
That all her very presence shed a light
Such as no waking eye-ball ever bore.
It was Herself, returned out of her Star,
More beautiful than earthly women are.

O ecstasy of eyes; then to my ears
Nay, to my very spirit, came the tone,
The voice so silent for so many years,
The inmost voice that spoke to me alone:
'The morning comes,' she said, 'the tempest thins.
Our Night is ended and our day begins...

Now, to our souls, this Fortune comes to be
That, within little space, as Time is told,
It will be granted that you come with me
To learn the wonders that these towers hold,
To let in light, to open all the doors,
To halls and stairs, to rooms and corridors.

Many and evil prisons lie below,
Things of old ill and murder in the night,
With chains in rust from blood shed long ago,
And broken tools from tortures of old spite.
But these are gone, their roofs are fallen in,
On paven ways our questings will begin.

Unknown to us the untrodden stairs and ways,
Unknown the darkness just beyond the bend,
Unknown the thing behind the door that sways,
Unknown the footsteps sensed as we ascend
We cannot know what dreads or glories be
Until we open, let in light, and see.

The will is in ourselves, that will attempt;
The keys are in ourselves that will unlock;
The prize is all fulfilment of dream dreamt,
Springs in Sahara, harvest amid rock,
Treasure on treasure to the will that drives
Despite of grief and hate through bitter lives.

This is the venture that awaits us here,
Exploring these two towers inly linked,
Both truly one, not two, as they appear,
But shadowed both till light make them distinct:
Distinct as on the summit of each one
Those pyramids of Apples of the Sun.

We, the disunioned two, who have long known
The soul's starvation, parted from a friend,
The emptiness of being all alone,
The daylong days, the nights that never end,
Now have reward, inestimable gain
Quest beyond price, with unity again.'

At this, her radiant beauty grew so bright,
The towers, with their pyramids, so glowed,
I could no longer see them for the light:
Light, and more light, through which no image showed;
The light that ended chaos, light that saves,
That brings the Spring and triumphs over graves.

Thus did she speak of happiness to be
Certainly, soon, ere many days were done,
Her very self at very one with me,
Impulse and purpose both at very one...
What more to say, but that I dearly wait
Commanding Death's tense whisper at the gate.

Here, then, I linger at my study fire,
About the lamp a moth is butting dim,
Without, the leaves fly at the wind's desire,
A tawny owl bewails the grief in him,
The quarter moon wests silver to the sea.
One hour more, and She will be with me.

from Grace Before Ploughing

Epilogue

Such is the living bread allowed,
(Should Fortune warrant), till a share
Rends all to tatters under cloud
With wrack and ruin everywhere,
As other fortune falls,
And buds are beaten bare.

In the unseen, in the unknown,
About us, planning, seeing, wise,
The Helpers comfort the alone
Through all that destinies devise.
Though waterless, in sand,
The buds break, being sown.

The Hopes that kindle man are true
The thought for others has reward,
Unseen, it makes the world anew,
Till loss regretted is restored,
And in man's darkest soul
The voiceless plea of love is harkened to.

from In Glad Thanksgiving

Remembering Dame Myra Hess

Most beautiful, most gifted, and most wise,
How shall man word the wonder that you were,
Now that your grace no longer blesses eyes,
Your presence nulls no care?
You are set free, as music that you played,
Made life a glory as your fingers bade,
You are alive with all that never dies.

For surely now you are among the rays
That guide and bless our darkness, as we grope
From wreck to ruin in life's tangled maze,
Lighting the paths of Hope…
Wisdom that sent you still directs your giving
The Courage that determines all things living
To seek for beauty and to light the ways.

I see you, as upon your stage alone,
In the great breathless silence that awaits
You, with the touches that make beauty known
Unbarring the shut gates…
You, the clear-eyed, who saw, in the attempt,
Eternal sparks illumine the dream dreamt,
The starry hand that scattered the seed sown.

For Luke O'Connor

One early Summer, when the times were bad,
In 'Little Old New York', long years ago,
I looked for work, an ignorant raw lad,
Knowing no craft, nor knowing how to know.

There, up and down, in the exciting Sun,
I offered help that no one seemed to need,
Then suddenly success came; Life had won;
Luke offered work, and I was saved indeed.

Saved and restarted, with the golden chance
(At last) of learning what mankind has wrought
In all his centuries of ignorance;
To light his darkness with the stars of thought.

These are belated thanks, but let me say,
'For seventy years I've thanked you every day.'

A Song of Waking

The stars are dim before the Sun has risen;
The sky they stell is as a windless lake
That seems to need a word, that seems to listen
For unheard order bidding morning break.
The word for the unlocking of the prison,
To bid the Sun arise and men awake.

Awake; the peacocks roosting on the boughs
Scream, and fly down, with scatterings of dew;
Up, in their cote the tumbler pigeons rouse,
A distant cock crows, and is answered-to.
The world is all awaking from its drowse,
To the day's trouble and the work to do.

Within the Tower, ringers' fingers grope
By lantern-light, and, at a word, their heaves,
Jangling awhile, bring music from the rope,
Startling the jackdaws nesting in the eaves.
The jangling stumbles into tune with Hope,
'Awake, and try, even if Death bereaves.'

Awake, for from the never-pastured whins,
The morning brings the light of a new day.
The Night is gone, the Morning re-begins,
Up, man, awake and ask what people say:
'Was there no room in any of the inns,
For other strangers who might show the way?'

Away, all pilgrims, to your pilgrimage,
Though the Sun shine not, you have still the light,
The Day unfolds, a fair, unwritten page,
Awakened hearts will tell you what to write,
And you the specks upon a starry stage
Have still a Day before the unknown Night.

Away, awake, before the day is old,
Somewhere, in every heart it's April still,
April with little lambkins out of fold,
The black-thorn and the yellow daffodil,
In mud by happy brooks, the marigold,
And married blackbird cocks with golden bill.

What The Wrekin Gave

You matchless two, to whom I owe
That comradeship of long ago,
Those times past praise,
That Sun, when all life else was snow,
You gladden all an old man's woe,
With joy that glows and stays.

Give Way

'Give way, my lads,' the coxwains used to say
Bossing the crew and thinking themselves clever,
'So toss her up and splash me not with spray...
Give way.'

Then, out across the Sloyne or down the bay
The cutter made the water walls dissever,
The seagulls mewed above us in their play.

All earthly ill surrenders to endeavour,
Every tomorrow is another day,
All irons that seem barriers for ever
Give way.

Old England

Just half a century since, an old man showed
Some photographs of forty years before,
Of timber carters in a country road
The very people, in the clothes they wore.

There they appeared; the nation now extinct,
Survivors from before the Flood they seemed,
Horses and carts such parts of them, so linked,
That they were one, a trinity undreamed.

A trinity in unity of power
To tomm the oak-tree into human use,
Or with a twitched ring make a bull to cower,
Or, grinning, turned the shire stallion loose.

Such might was in them they were hardly men,
Those prehistorics peopling England then.

Miscellaneous Verse, 1930–1967

['They buried him...']

They buried him, and then the soldiers slept;
The city feasted; and the feasters told
How all the crucifyings had been done.

But before dawn the heavy stone unrolled,
The grave-clothes fell, the Living Form outstept.
Man's many-millioned darkness knew the sun.

We are all buried deep. Arise! Arise!
In us, O Living Form, out of this hate,
This greed, this night, this starving in the stone.

Roll back the self-shut boulders of our fate,
That we may know our power and be wise
In the light for ever about us truly known.

[*The Form and Order of the Service... of the Ceremonies that are to be
observed in the Foundation of the Dean and Chapter of the Cathedral
Church of Christ, Liverpool* (Liverpool: The Church Press, 1931),
p. 11]

[Ode on the Opening of the Shakespeare Memorial Theatre]

Beside this House there is a blackened shell,
The theatre that Flower built of old,
Lest English love of Shakespeare should grow cold.
He, Stratford's citizen, established here
A home for Shakespeare, that for many a year
Drew happy thousands till the fire befell.
I saw its ruins, black in smoke that rolled.

Now a new House has risen: it is given
Not by one citizen or state: it stands
Given to us by many hundred hands
American and British: nay, each race
Upon this earth has helped to build this place
Lovers of Shakespeare everywhere have striven
Every man gave it out of all earth's lands.

First, let us thank the givers for the gift,
This consecrated gift of brick and stone,
Where Poetry the Queen shall have her throne.
Long may the givers come here to unite
With us, in Shakespeare's service of delight –
The acted passion beautiful and swift,
The spirit leaping out of flesh and bone.

And may this House be famous, may it be
The home of lovely players: and a stage
Schooling young poets to a fruitful age.
We but begin, our story is not told:
Friends, may this day begin an age of gold,
England again a star among the sea,
That beauty hers that is her heritage.

[*The Times*, 25 April 1932, p. 15]

To Rudyard Kipling

Your very heart was England's; it is just
That England's very heart should keep your dust.

[*The Times*, 23 January 1936, p. 13]

For the Men of the Merchant Navy and Fishing Fleets

They dare all weathers in all climes and seas
In every kind of ship; the risks they run
Are all the greatest underneath the sun.
Their Fortune is as flinty as their bread.

Some truces Nature grants them, never peace;
The work they do is hourly undone.
By them, we make our money and are fed,
Let England, doing Justice, honour these.

[*Merchant Navy Week*… (Portsmouth: Gale and Polden, 1937), p. 7]

Neville Chamberlain

As Priam to Achilles for his Son,
So you, into the night, divinely led,
To ask that young men's bodies, not yet dead,
Be given from the battle not begun.

[*The Times*, 16 September 1938, p. 13]

The Many and the Man

The brisk and prosperous and clever people,
The educated and the ruling class,
Unanimously said, 'He is an ass;
Bees in his bonnet; jackdaws in his steeple.'

The Doctors said, 'He isn't mad; but odd.'
Societies for Birds and Beasts, though loath,
Summoned him up, for cruelties to both.
The Church deplored his attitude to God.

With pity and contempt men stopped to look;
With missiles and abuse boys stayed to mock;
But still the vessel prospered in the dock,
As Noah, plank by plank, the gopher took.

The weather-prophets said, 'He isn't sane.'
The Herd, as ever, pressed upon its Man...
And then, a month after the rain began,
Wisdom approved him... it began to RAIN.

[*Survey Graphic* – '*Calling America*' (New York: Harper and
Brothers, 1939), p. 31]

Red Cross

I remember a moonless night in a blasted town,
And the cellar-steps with their army-blanket-screen,
And the stretcher-bearers, groping and stumbling down
To the Red Cross struggle with Death in the ill-lit scene.

There, entering-in, I saw, at a table near,
A surgeon tense by a man who struggled for breath.
A shell, that shattered above us, rattled the gear,
The dying one looked at me, as if I were Death.

He died, and was borne away, and the surgeon wept;
An elderly man, well-used, as one would have thought
To western war and the revels that Death then kept:
Why weep for one when a million ranked as naught?

He said, 'We have buried heaps since the push began.
From now to the Peace we'll bury a thousand more.
It's silly to cry, but I could have saved that man
Had they only carried him in an hour before.'

[*The Queen's Book of the Red Cross* (London: Hodder and Stoughton, 1939), p. 29]

[*'In the black Maytime…'*]

In the black Maytime when we faced the worst
And saw the punishment that Nature deals
To Nations ranking fat unwisdom first,
And the iron Judge rejected all appeals,
Then, when no other human light appeared,
And men surmised the bitter truth untold,
That we were lost, and that disaster neared,
To rank us with the empires lost of old,
Then, comfort came, for suddenly we knew
A forethought and a courage and a skill
Descending out of Heaven from a few
To smite aside the certainty of ill,
And Hope returned, and those we longed to save
Were given Life and lifted from the grave.

[*The Twenty Five Days* (London: William Heinemann Ltd., 1941) [proof copy], p. 213]

['Let a people reading stories…']

Let a people reading stories full of anguish
Showing mighty Nations humbled by a blindness,
By a want of wisdom, scorn or hate of knowledge,
Insolence in office,
Emptiness of mind or indolence in office,
Cringing to the false one and the true denying,
Boasting of the self-gift while the un-self scorning,
Anything save labour,
Let them recollect that bright Imagination
Smiting with her sun-flash will, like hosts of angels,
Shine so that her hundreds pluck the many millions
Even from disaster.

[*The Twenty Five Days* (London: William Heinemann Ltd., 1941)
[proof copy], p. 215]

['Walking the darkness…']

Walking the darkness, far from home, at midnight,
Sometimes I see them, lighted at the wing-tips,
The cockpits winking with the spark of signals,
The outbound bombers.

My thought perceives them switch away the sidelights
And cease to signal as they drive to danger,
From England, over sea, to blackened Europe
Where fire awaits them.

I say, 'O come home safely, midnight darers,
And may a day dawn when the youths of nations
Will hold like purpose, striving to make perfect
The life that binds us.'

[William Rothenstein, *Men of the R.A.F.* (Oxford: University Press, 1942), p. 85]

233

Now

Will moonèd Fortune make the tide to turn?
Does reckoning begin on those whose crime,
In insolence, put back the clock of Time,
To make the World's Soul squalid as their own?

Where the killed victims are, what flags are flown?

What prospect is, that from our banded few,
Pledged unto Death, Earth's quiet will ensue?

The men go forward to a Fate unknown…
O Fortune, spill a brightness from thy urn.

[*The Manchester Guardian*, 7 June 1944, p. 4]

The Ambulance Ship[.] Port of London Authority
A Morning Drill

We passed through canyons of a Carthage dead;
No work of man was in those narrow ways
Skulled on by blackened windows without glaze;
Warehouse and ware had gone; War's Sunday held.
War had made yester-noonday look like eld
And penny-grabbing a forgotten craze;
To-morrow might be: Yesterday was sped.

Acres we passed, war-weathered into crags:
Then there were sea-gulls mewing in a reach,
Three-quarter ebb, with barges on the beach,
And over them more eyeless, crownless shells
Of ruins like to belfries without bells
With splintered ends of girders stuck from each
And rubble tumbled on the wharfing flags.

234

And lo, a river-ship was at the Pier,
Steam up and colours flying, as before
When, round the bending in the Berkshire shore
She crept, in Summer, driving flocking waves
Into the brook-rats' and the otters' caves,
Exactly timed, five minutes before four,
Beside the very watcher present here.

Within that past of Peace her rows of chairs
Peopled with merriment and holiday,
Advanced, all eyes, above a flash of spray,
Silent, all faces on the railing hung,
Until abreast, when every boy gave tongue
With ribaldry of comment and Hurray.
War gave her crew another zest than theirs.

Now, under War, another order shewed:
The noble bareness to which seamen strip
The work- and living-quarters of a ship,
Was made a ring, for battling death and dirt.
Now, every space held mercy for the hurt,
That cleanliness and hope might come to grip
With every devil loosed from hell's abode.

In light and spotlessness the beds were ranged,
The stretchers were prepared, the windows freed
To pass the wounded through in case of need;
The hempen slings lay ready on the deck
For lifting bodies round protruding wreck;
To each imagined ill, forethoughtful heed,
Sea discipline by loving kindness changed.

There stood the men and women of the crew.
Would that I had their portraits painted here,
Those faces of devotion, courage, cheer,
Each, in its way, an image of our best,
Each, always, daily making someone blest
By bringing hope and putting away fear
And shining out with life when murder flew.

Doubtless, those valiants in the topsied world
Had seen the sack well-shaken by event,
Had neighboured Death, and known what danger meant
From ice and sun, and ocean storm-bedevilled,
Here, they had seen the granite coping levelled,
The city spire into shivers sent
And the bright weathercock to the gutters hurled.

They had seen half the river walled with flame,
The running fire making midnight bright,
The gun- and bomb-blasts shattering the night,
And many hundred foemen in the air.
Had the patrol-boat bringing orders there
Called them to such a testing of their might
Instead of drill, it would have been the same.

They stood across the river to the side
Of grounded barges, over which the bank
Towered, with skeletons of stone in rank,
Warehouse on gutted warehouse, gaunt and bleak,
The tilings of their roofs in sloping peak
Showed on the ground through windows broken blank.
I clambered to the wharf-top with my guide.

Then in the courts of ruin blasted bare
Upon the wharves, long starved of any bale,
To crowds of all the children within hail,
They rigged the sheers, by which, securely slung,
Stretcher by stretcher, volunteers were swung
Down to the barges overthwart the rail,
And thence below-decks to the surgeon's care.

All things conspired to create delight,
The sun, the lapsing stream, the wondrous crew,
Their welcome to the order that I knew,
The spotlessness their effort had achieved
In simple practice of a faith believed,
Their triumph over aught that ill could do,
The nobleness that made their faces bright,

So that, on coming thence, the scenes remained
Lively and lovely in the spirit's cell,
As some bright story, difficult to tell,
Which, being fitly told, is as a sun
Illumining the heart in everyone,
Making the sullen glad, the sorry, well,
The frustrate, happy with delight attained.

And though the milling of the stones of war
May grind from living spirits through the year
A grist of curses in each hemisphere
A blasting moistened by no human spring,
This in my mind is as a deathless thing
A cock in deepest darkness crowing cheer,
That brightness will return, and will restore.

[*Soho Centenary* (London: Hutchinson & Co. Ltd., [1944]), pp. 9–11

For All Seafarers

Even in peace, scant quiet is at sea;
In war, each revolution of the screw,
Each breath of air that blows the colours free,
May be the last life movement known to you.

Death, thrusting up or down, may disunite
Spirit from body, purpose from the hull,
With thunder, bringing leaving of the light,
With lightning letting nothingness annul.

No rock, no danger, bears a warning sign,
No lighthouse scatters welcome through the dark;
Above the sea, the bomb; afloat, the mine;
Beneath, the gangs of the torpedo-shark.

Year after year, with insufficient guard,
Often with none, you have adventured thus;
Some, reaching harbour, maimed and battle-scarred,
Some, never more returning, lost to us.

But, if you 'scape, tomorrow, you will steer
To peril once again, to bring us bread,
To dare again, beneath the sky of fear,
The moon-moved graveyard of your brothers dead.

You were salvation to the army lost,
Trapped, but for you, upon the Dunkirk beach;
Death barred the way to Russia, but you crosst;
To Crete and Malta, but you succoured each.

Unrecognized, you put us in your debt;
Unthanked, you enter, or escape, the grave;
Whether your land remember or forget
You saved the land, or died to try to save.

[*Merchantmen at War* (London: His Majesty's Stationery Office, 1944), p. 5]

A Moment Comes

Now that the murderers are put away
(At cost of the world's hope), a moment comes,
Not feverish with war-cries, flags and drums,
Not terrible with terror and dismay,
Not beautiful (the lovely hope being dead),
Not hopeful, therefore, but... the time arrives...
A moment when the wax of human lives
May take, for nobler seal, a lovelier head.

Is it too grim a burden, to maintain
A will, that murder shall not rule again?
That bloody man shall cage, like bloody beast?
Man must not make less beauty than the flower.
Youth, given back from slaughter, has an hour.
Lighten us, Life: shine, planet, in our east.

[*The Times*, 8 May 1945, p. 7]

On the Ninetieth Birthday of Bernard Shaw

After these ninety years, he can survey
Changes enough, so many due to him:–
Old wax-work melted down, old tinsel dim,
Old sentimental clock-work put away.

There the old playthings with their lovers lie;
But he remains, the bright mind ever young,
The glorious great heart, the witty tongue,
Erasing Shaw, who made the folly die.

Is there a cranny in our old conceit
Unlightened by the brightness of his mind?
Is there a blinker, making many blind,
Unrent by him, to show that light is sweet?

Is there a mystery in life or fate
To which his spirit has not sought a door?
Is there a play, in all his pungent store,
Not touching home? unlinked with something great?

Honour him living, all Earth's brightest brains.
Let Ministers of Fine Arts, centuries hence,
Order him statues; let us have more sense,
And call a splendour great while he remains.

[S. Winsten (ed.), *G.B.S. 90* (London: Hutchinson and Co., 1946), p. 17]

Franklin Delano Roosevelt

Honour this man, so stricken in his prime,
So shattered in his life's most kindling years,
That had his spirit not been strong as Time
He could have won no tribute more than tears.

Honour a dauntless soul and golden voice
(None sweeter ever spoke in Christian lands)
Through him, the horror passed, and we rejoice,
Our countries are released, and Freedom stands.

[*The Times*, 12 April 1948, p. 5]

A Hope for the Newly-Born

May destiny, allotting what befalls,
Grant to the newly-born this saving grace,
A guard more sure than ships and fortress-walls,
The loyal love and service of a race.

[*The Times*, 16 November 1948, p. 5]

[The Laying of the Foundation Stone of The National Theatre]

Here we lay stone, that, at a future time,
May bear a House, wherein, in days to be,
Tier upon tier, delighted crowds may see
Men's passions made a plaything, and sublime.

240

Here, fellowships of lovers of the arts
May work together, to create anew
Worlds, that a poet in his rapture knew,
Fairer than this, our hell of broken hearts.

Pray, therefore, brothers, as we put the stone,
That glory from the Never-Dying-Mind
May triumph here, with vision for the blind,
Making joy daily bread, and beauty known.

[*The Times*, 14 July 1951, p. 4]

On the Birthday of a Great Man

This Man, in darkness, saw; in doubtings, led;
In danger, did; in uttermost despair,
Shone, with a Hope that made the midnight fair.
The world he saved calls blessing on his head.

[*The Times*, 30 November 1954, p. 9]

On Coming Towards Eighty

The Unchanging

The marvels do not lessen as years pass;
The Evening Star still ushers in her night,
The daisies remain wonders in the grass,
The sky-larks still enchant from out of sight.

There are the Downs, so difficult to paint,
In exquisite sweet curves, so vast, so fair,
Now crested with a beech-clump; anon, faint,
Dim, distant, blue, exactly as they were.

Solemn, with ancient hawthorn trees, as erst,
Icknield and Ridge Ways pass the windy wold.
The brook-lime blossoms where the chalk-springs burst;
The bird cries thrill my being as of old: –

The unseen plovers, calling for the Spring;
The curlews, laugh-lamenting, on the wing.

The Changing

How wondrously life changes as it goes;
Within this life how England has been changed
To something of her ancient sign, a Rose,
Where, lately, squalor and starvation ranged.

The ragged, foodless, untaught hordes are gone,
A Hope is springing from the old despair.
The strength is here; if Beauty lead us on
We may leave living land-marks everywhere.

Whatever we attain to, men can say: –
'Those people, once so wealthy and so proud,
Determined that their race should have today,
Fed, clad, enlightened, and with heads unbowed.

Within a life-time, effort made it so.
Heaven is for all who have the will to go.'

[[*The Times* Bookshop], *John Masefield* (London: The Times
Bookshop, 1958), pp. 10–11]

In Memory of Alfred Edward Housman

Born March 26, 1859

Too many lads of pith and relish
Who put their all in pledge,
Find Love a hell and living hellish
Twixt Clun and Wenlock Edge.

Cureless are broken hearts and breaking,
They ache; but here was one
Who made a music of the aching
Twixt Wenlock Edge and Clun.

[*The Times*, 26 March 1959, p. 13]

Words to the Speakers of Poetry

Remember, as you read a poet's page
That, often, as he wrote, his spirit bled
From hate and envy throughout youth and age,
That this might gladden mortals, he being dead.

Within his work, in symbols of picked words
Are Heaven and Earth, and all that man perceives,
Stars, oceans, mountains, angels, beasts and birds,
And Destiny, that blesses or bereaves.

So, speak no poem till it make such a glow
Within your spirit that the truth is bared;
Then, it will speak through you, and you will know
How little can be Heaven until shared.

[Copy in John Masefield's hand, written for Kay Barmby, March 1960. Transcribed by Constance Babington Smith. From The John Masefield Society CBS Archive (interviews folder)]

To the Great Friends in Lifetime

This, I believe, that we remain in Time
Holding the purpose of a quest incurred
Outlasting Death, to struggle and to climb
Mountainous Life with living deed or word,
Achieving light (if lucky) out of grime.
So, when Life's breath has gone,
Aspiring spirit smiles, and ventures on.

Newly arrayed, the spirit re-assails
Despairs unconquered in the past, and longs
For fellow treaders on the ancient trails
Loved in the past's forgotten toils and songs,
Old friends, linked by old chain
Re-met, are welcomed and are friends again
Exultingly the old ship spreads her sails.

Naught that is living can the soul forget.
Companions now were helpers in the past
Erasing blottings, nullifying debt.
Lovely, all lacks secured,
Attended, recreated, reassured,
Manful, in life more hopeful than the last,
Onward the great soul goes to greater yet.

*   *   *   *

Never has such assumption seemed more true
Than now, when lovely spirits, lost to sight,
In memory return
Nearer than ever to the hearts that yearn,
Giving again the happiness they knew,
Reviving occupations of delight
And winning, all too late, the praises due.

That we are linked in long-established schemes
Is, still, my thought; and so
That we shall meet again I dearly know,
Under the tidal moon, swayed by the sun.
Darkness besets man's living with its dreams,
Eternity from mortal conquest streams,
Joy, Order, Peace and Wisdom's Justice done.

[Corliss Lamont (ed.), *The Thomas Lamont Family* (New York: Horizon Press, 1962), pp. 229–30]

John Fitzgerald Kennedy

All generous hearts lament the leader killed,
The young chief with the smile, the radiant face,
The winning way that turned a wondrous race
Into sublimer pathways, leading on.

Grant to us Life that though the man be gone
The promise of his spirit be fulfilled.

[*The Times*, 25 November 1963, p. 11]

East Coker

Here, whence his forbears sprang, a man is laid
As dust, in quiet earth, whose written word
Helped many thousands broken and dismayed
Among the ruins of triumphant wrong.
May many an English flower and little bird
(Primrose and robin redbreast unafraid)
Gladden this garden where his rest is made
And Christmas song respond, and Easter song.

[*The Times*, 8 January 1965, p. 11]

Sir Winston Churchill

The Divine Fortune, watching Life's affairs,
Justly endowed him with what Fortune may,
With sense of Storm and where the Centre lay,
With tact of deed, in some wise witty way,

Fortune of parents came in equal shares,
With England's wisest mingling with the West,
A startling newness, making better best,
A newness putting old things to a test...

So, when convulsion came, and direst need,
When, in a mess of Nations overthrown,
This England stood at bay, and stood alone,
His figure, then commanding, stood as stone,

Or, speaking, uttered like the very breed
Of Francis Drake, disaster being near,
One solemn watchword, to have done with fear.
Thence, without other drum-beat, all took cheer,
Content with such a Captain, such a Creed.

[*The Times*, 25 January 1965, p. 13]

[On Swinburne]

The lines I scribble here are weak,
But not unblest has been my doom.
I heard the poet Swinburne speak,
In the Museum Reading Room.

[Private Collection (PWE), dated 16 November 1966]

Remembering Dame Myra Hess

Glad memories come, of old, long-distant days
When I, with many hundreds, saw and heard,
And joined with many hundreds in her praise,
Glad memories, all, with no remembered word,
But with the sense that she who played perceived
The world undying, that composers know
At moments, as reward for years of woe,
She touched that deathless world and we believed.

Death to such souls is as a night in May
When a small bird's ecstatic throat declares
Beauty undying to the moonlit airs
Blending both Death and Night in deathless day.

[Howard Ferguson (ed.), *Myra Hess By Her Friends* (London: Hamish
Hamilton, 1966), p. 1]

Sources

Salt-Water Ballads. London: Grant Richards, 1902:
  'A Consecration' (pp. 1–2); 'Burial Party' (pp. 11–13); 'Bill' (p. 14); 'Fever Ship' (pp. 15–16); 'Hell's Pavement' (pp. 25–6); 'Sea-Change' (pp. 27–8); 'Harbour-Bar' (pp. 29–30); 'Nicias Moriturus' (pp. 31–2); 'A Night at Dago Tom's' (pp. 38–9); "Port o' Many Ships" (pp. 40–1); 'Mother Carey' (pp. 48–9); 'Trade Winds' (p. 58); 'Sea-Fever' (pp. 59–60); 'A Wanderer's Song' (pp. 61–2); 'Cardigan Bay' (p. 63); 'The Tarry Buccaneer' (pp. 68–70); 'A Ballad of John Silver' (pp. 71–3); 'The West Wind' (pp. 79–81); 'Sorrow o' Mydath' (p. 84); 'Vagabond' (p. 85); 'Spunyarn' (p. 88); 'Personal' (p. 91); 'On Eastnor Knoll' (p. 96); "All Ye That Pass By" (pp. 99–100); 'In Memory of A.P.R.' (p. 101)
Ballads. London: Elkin Mathews, 1903:
  'The Ballad of Sir Bors' (pp. 9–11); 'Spanish Waters' (pp. 12–17); 'Cargoes' (pp. 18–19); 'Captain Stratton's Fancy' (pp. 20–2); 'St Mary's Bells' (pp. 25–6); 'London Town' (pp. 27–30); 'The Emigrant' (pp. 31–2); 'The Seekers' (pp. 37–9); 'Hall Sands' (pp. 40–2); 'Laugh and be Merry' (pp. 44–5); 'Blind Man's Vigil' (pp. 46–8); 'Roadways' (pp. 49–50)
A Mainsail Haul. London: Elkin Mathews, 1905:
  ['I yarned with ancient shipmen...'] (p. 5)
Ballads [second edition]. London: Elkin Mathews, 1910:
  'Twilight' (pp. 59–60)
Ballads and Poems. London: Elkin Mathews, 1910:
  'Posted as Missing' (pp. 62–3); 'A Creed' (pp. 64–6); 'When Bony Death' (pp. 67–8); 'Being Her Friend' (p. 73); 'Fragments' (pp. 74–8); 'The Death Rooms' (pp. 82–3); 'C.L.M.' (pp. 89–90); 'Waste' (p. 91); 'Third Mate' (pp. 92–3); 'Christmas, 1903' (pp. 98–9); 'The Word' (p. 100)
The Street of To-Day. London: J.M. Dent, 1911:
  ['O beauty, I have wandered far...'] (p. vii)
Miscellaneous Verse, 1899–1911
  'Sonnet – To the Ocean' (*The Bookman*, Vol. XLVIII No. 5, New York: George H. Doran, January 1919, p. 546); [Before Beginning] (Bodleian. Dep.c.314); 'Theodore' (*A Broad Sheet*. No. 19, July 1903); ['Oh some are fond of cow's milk...'] (Bodleian. MS.Eng.poet.d.194, ff.16–17); 'Theodore to his Mother' (Bodleian. MS.Eng.poet.d.194, f.6); 'Vallipo' (*The Manchester Guardian*, 14 November 1904, p. 5); 'The Gara Brook' (*The Manchester Guardian*, 18 November 1904, p. 5); 'Westward Ho' (*The Manchester Guardian*, 26 November 1904, p. 7); 'The Whale' (*A Sailor's Garland*. London: Methuen & Co., 1906, pp. 178–80); 'The Salcombe Seaman's Flaunt to the Proud Pirate' (*A Sailor's Garland*. London: Methuen & Co., 1906, pp. 293–4); 'Campeachy Picture' (*A Broadside*. No. 1. Dundrum, Co. Dublin: Dun Emer Press, June 1908, pp. 1–2); 'Theodore to his Grandson' (*A Broadside*. No. 8. Dundrum, Co. Dublin: Cuala Press, January 1909, p. 1); 'By a Bier-Side' (*The Englishwoman*. No. 3. April 1909, p. 236); 'Chorus' (*The Englishwoman*. No. 7. August 1909, p. 41); [The Pirate Poet on the *Monte*] (Jack B. Yeats. *A Little Fleet*. London: Elkin Mathews, [1909] pp. 9–10)
The Everlasting Mercy. London: Sidgwick and Jackson, 1911:
  'Saul Kane's Madness' (pp. 28–41); ['O lovely lily clean...'] (p. 90)

The Widow in the Bye Street. London: Sidgwick and Jackson, 1912:
   [The Ending] (pp. 95–97)
Dauber. London: William Heinemann, 1913:
   ['Denser it grew…'] (pp. 54–7); 'We Therefore Commit Our Brother' (pp. 88–92)
Philip the King and other poems. London: William Heinemann, 1914:
   'Truth' (pp. 59–60); 'The *Wanderer*' (pp. 61–71); 'August, 1914' (pp. 72–5); [Extract I from 'Biography'] (p. 76); [Extract II from 'Biography'] (p. 86); 'They Closed Her Eyes' (pp. 96–100)
The Faithful. London: William Heinemann, 1915:
   [Kurano's Song] (pp. 86–7)
Good Friday. Letchworth: Garden City Press Limited, 1916:
   ['They cut my face…'] (pp. 39–40); ['The wild duck…'] (pp. 47–50); ['Only a penny…'] (pp. 76–7)
Sonnets and Poems. Letchworth: Garden City Press, 1916:
   'V' (p. 9); 'VI' (p. 10); 'VII' (p. 11); 'VIII' (p. 12); 'IX' (p. 13); 'X' (p. 14); 'XI' (p. 15); 'XII' (p. 16); 'XIII' (p. 17); 'XIV' (p. 18); 'XV' (p. 19); 'XVI' (p. 20); 'XVII' (p. 21); 'XIX' (p. 23); 'XX' (p. 24); 'XXVI' (p. 30); 'XXX' (p. 34); 'XXXIII' (p. 37); 'XXXVII' (p. 41); 'XXXVIII' (p. 42); 'XL' (p. 44); 'XLI' (p. 45); 'XLII' (p. 46); 'XLIV' (p. 48); 'XLVII' (p. 51)
Sonnets and Poems. Lollingdon: John Masefield, 1916:
   'XXXIV' (p. 38); 'XXXV' (p. 39); 'XXXVI' (pp. 40–1)
Gallipoli. London: William Heinemann, 1916:
   'Epilogue' (p. 183)
Salt-Water Poems and Ballads. New York: Macmillan, 1916:
   'The New Bedford Whaler' (p. 123)
Lollingdon Downs and other poems, with sonnets. London: William Heinemann, 1917:
   'III' (p. 4); 'V' (p. 6); 'VI' (p. 7); 'VII' (p. 8); 'IX' (p. 11); 'X' (p. 12); 'XI' (p. 13); 'XXIV' (pp. 43–4)
Reynard the Fox. London: William Heinemann, 1919:
   ['The fox was strong…'] (pp. 86–7); ['And here, as he ran to the huntsman's yelling…'] (pp. 97–8); 'The End of the Run' (pp. 118–24)
Enslaved and other poems. London: William Heinemann, 1920:
   [Gerard's Answer] (pp. 59–61); 'Sonnets' (pp. 101–4); 'The Lemmings' (p. 121); 'On Growing Old' (pp. 123–4)
Right Royal. London: William Heinemann, 1920:
   ['As a whirl of notes…'] (pp. 108–9)
King Cole. London: William Heinemann, 1921:
   'King Cole Speaks' (p. 30)
Miscellaneous Verse, 1911–1921
   'Die We Must' (*A Broadside.* No.12 (Fourth Year). Dundrum, Co. Dublin: Cuala Press, May 1912, p. 1); 'The Gara River' (*A Broadside.* No. 3 (Sixth Year). Dundrum, Co. Dublin: Cuala Press, August 1913, p. 2); 'Skyros' (from letter to Edward Marsh, 16 October [1915]) (Berg Collection, The New York Public Library)
King Cole and other poems. London: William Heinemann, 1923:
   'The Rider at the Gate' (pp. 71–3); 'The Haunted' (pp. 84–90)
Odtaa. London: William Heinemann, 1926:
   'The Meditation of Highworth Ridden' (p. 343)

The Midnight Folk. London: William Heinemann, 1927:
  [Not a Nice Song by Rollicum Bitem] (pp. 29–30); [Miss Piney Tricker] (p. 142); [The Wind] (p. 195); [Naggy] (p. 295)
The Coming of Christ. London: William Heinemann, 1928:
  [Song of the Chorus] (pp. 19–21]
Midsummer Night and other tales in verse. London: William Heinemann, 1928:
  'The Begetting of Arthur' (pp. 2–13); 'Midsummer Night' (pp. 78–86); 'Dust to Dust' (p. 152)
Any Dead to Any Living. New Haven: The Yale Review, 1928
  'Any Dead to Any Living' (p. 3)
Miscellaneous Verse, 1922–1930
  'The Racer' (*The Racer*, [Oxford: John Masefield, 1922], (privately printed poetry card)); 'St Felix School' (*St Felix School Southwold 1897–1923*. London: Chelsea Publishing Co., [1923], p. 5); ['On these three things a poet must depend…'] (HRHRC. MS (Masefield, J.) Works [Untitled poem] 'On these three things a poet must depend…'); 'Lines on Sea Adventure' (Basil Lubbock, *Adventures by Sea from Art of Old Time*. London: The Studio, 1925, pp. 1–3); 'Polyxena's Speech' (*The Oxford Recitations*. New York: Macmillan Company, 1928, pp. 47–9)
The Wanderer of Liverpool. London: William Heinemann, 1930:
  'Adventure On' (*A Book of Both Sorts*. London: William Heinemann, 1947, pp. 191–2 (adapted from 'The Ending', *The Wanderer of Liverpool*. London: William Heinemann, 1930)); 'Liverpool, 1890' (p. 105); 'Liverpool, 1930' (p. 106); 'Pay' (p. 110); 'Eight Bells' (p. 113); 'Posted' (p. 114); 'If' (p. 115)
Minnie Maylow's Story and other tales and scenes. London: William Heinemann, 1931:
  'Son of Adam' (pp. 22–31)
A Tale of Troy. London: William Heinemann, 1932:
  'The Horse' (pp. 20–2)
The Conway. London: William Heinemann, 1933:
  'After Forty Years' (p. 19)
The Box of Delights. London: William Heinemann, 1935:
  [Old Rum-Chops' Song] (p. 128)
Victorious Troy. London: William Heinemann, 1935:
  ['When the last captives…'] (p. 298)
A Letter from Pontus and other verse. London: William Heinemann, 1936:
  'Ballet Russe' (pp. 27–8); 'February Night' (p. 43); 'Wood–Pigeons' (pp. 68–9); 'Autumn Ploughing' (p. 70); 'Partridges' (p. 74); 'The Towerer' (pp. 75–6); 'The Eyes' (p. 78); 'Porto Bello' (pp. 83–4); 'A Ballad of Sir Francis Drake' (pp. 88–90); 'The *Mayblossom*' (pp. 91–3); 'Sweet Friends' (p. 109)
The Country Scene. London: William Collins, 1937:
  'On England' (pp. 9–10); 'Lambing' (p. 18); 'Nomads' (p. 22); 'The Gallop on the Sands' (p. 24); 'The Morris Dancers' (p. 30); 'The Mare and Foal at Grass' (p. 36); 'The County Show' (p. 38); 'Elephants in the Tent' (p. 40); 'The Roadside Inn' (p. 44); 'The Procession of the Bulls' (p. 46); 'The Tight-rope Walker' (p. 52); 'Their Canvas Home' (p. 54); 'The Horse and Trap at the Ford' (p. 60); 'The Horse in the Barn' (p. 66); 'The Ploughing Match' (p. 82); 'Hunting' (p. 84); 'Timber Hauling' (p. 90); 'The Gipsies in the Snow' (p. 96)
Tribute to Ballet. London: William Collins, 1938:
  'The Foreign Dancers' (pp. 11–12); 'The Indian Dancers' (pp. 13–14); 'The

Class' (pp. 22–3); 'Rehearsal' (pp. 25–6); 'The Seventh Hungarian Dance of Brahms' (p. 32); 'Masks' (p. 33); 'Where They Took Train' (p. 37); 'The Painter of the Scene' (p. 41); 'Not Only the Most Famous' (p. 45)

Some Memories of W.B. Yeats. Dublin: Cuala Press, 1940:
'On His Tobacco Jar' (pp. 14–17); ['Willy's Geese…'] (p. 29)

The Nine Days Wonder. London: William Heinemann, 1941:
'Thoughts for Later On' (*The Twenty Five Days.* London: William Heinemann Ltd., 1941 [proof copy], pp. 213–14 and titled within *The Nine Days Wonder.* London: William Heinemann Ltd., 1941, p. 60)

A Generation Risen. London: William Collins, 1942:
'The Paddington Statue' (p. 8); 'The Station' (pp. 10–12); 'Paddington. Mother and Son' (p. 14); 'Two Soldiers Waiting' (p. 16); 'Sentries' (p. 22); 'Crews Coming Down Gangways' (p. 40)

On the Hill. London: William Heinemann, 1949:
'Blown Hilcote Manor' (pp. 39–40); 'The Wind of the Sea' (p. 113)

The Bluebells and other verse. London: William Heinemann, 1961:
'A Cry to Music' (p. 121); 'The Strange Case of Captain Barnaby' (pp. 200–5)

Old Raiger and other verse. London: William Heinemann, 1964:
'Jane' (p. 28); 'Pawn to Bishop's Five' (pp. 29–33); 'Lines for the Race of Sailing Ships…' (pp. 60–1); 'King Gaspar and his Dream' (pp. 70–3)

Grace Before Ploughing. London: William Heinemann, 1966:
'Epilogue' (p. 90)

In Glad Thanksgiving. London: William Heinemann, [1967]:
'Remembering Dame Myra Hess' (p. 1); 'For Luke O'Connor' (p. 2); 'A Song of Waking' (pp. 4–5); 'What The Wrekin Gave' (p. 7); 'Give Way' (p. 49); 'Old England' (p. 55)

Miscellaneous Verse, 1930–1967
['They buried him…'] (*…Foundation of the Dean and Chapter of the Cathedral Church of Christ Liverpool…* Liverpool: The Church Press, 1931, p. 11); [Ode on the Opening of the Shakespeare Memorial Theatre] (*The Times.* 25 April 1932, p. 15); 'To Rudyard Kipling' (*The Times.* 23 January 1936, p. 13); 'For the Men of the Merchant Navy and Fishing Fleets' (*Merchant Navy Week…* Portsmouth: Gale and Polden, 1937, p. 7); 'Neville Chamberlain' (*The Times.* 16 September 1938, p. 13); 'The Many and the Man' (*Survey Graphic – 'Calling America'*, New York: Harper and Brothers, 1939, p. 31); 'Red Cross' (*The Queen's Book of the Red Cross.* London: Hodder and Stoughton, 1939, p. 29); ['In the black Maytime…'] (*The Twenty Five Days.* London: William Heinemann Ltd., 1941 [proof copy], p. 213); ['Let a people reading stories…'] (*The Twenty Five Days.* London: William Heinemann Ltd., 1941 [proof copy], p. 215); ['Walking the darkness…'] (William Rothenstein, *Men of the R.A.F.* Oxford: University Press, 1942, p. 85); 'Now' (*The Manchester Guardian*, 7 June 1944, p. 4); 'The Ambulance Ship…' (*Soho Centenary.* London: Hutchinson & Co. Ltd., [1944], pp. 9–11); 'For All Seafarers' (*Merchantmen at War.* London: His Majesty's Stationery Office, 1944, p. 5); 'A Moment Comes' (*The Times.* 8 May 1945, p. 7); 'On the Ninetieth Birthday of Bernard Shaw' (ed. S. Winsten. *G.B.S. 90.* London: Hutchinson and Co., 1946, p. 17); 'Franklin Delano Roosevelt' (*The Times.* 12 April 1948, p. 5); 'A Hope for the Newly-Born' (*The Times.* 16 November 1948, p. 5); [The Laying of the Foundation Stone of The National Theatre] (*The Times.* 14 July 1951, p. 4); 'On the Birthday of a Great

Man' (*The Times*. 30 November 1954, p. 9); 'On Coming Towards Eighty' ([*The Times* Bookshop], *John Masefield*. London: The Times Bookshop, 1958, pp. 10–11); 'In Memory of Alfred Edward Housman' (*The Times*. 26 March 1959, p. 13); 'Words to the Speakers of Poetry' (transcribed by Constance Babington Smith. From The John Masefield Society Constance Babington Smith Archive (interviews folder)); 'To The Great Friends in Lifetime' (ed. Corliss Lamont. *The Thomas Lamont Family*. New York: Horizon Press, 1962, pp. 229–30); 'John Fitzgerald Kennedy' (*The Times*, 25 November 1963, p. 11); 'East Coker' (*The Times*. 8 January 1965, p. 11); 'Sir Winston Churchill' (*The Times*, 25 January 1965, p. 13); [On Swinburne] (Private Collection (PWE) dated 16 November 1966]; 'Remembering Dame Myra Hess' (ed. Howard Ferguson, *Myra Hess By Her Friends*. London: Hamish Hamilton, 1966, p. 1)

Index of First Lines

I yarned with ancient shipmen beside the galley range,	30
I'm going to be a pirate with a bright brass pivot-gun,	12
If all be governed by the moving stars,	96
If Beauty be at all, if, beyond sense,	100
If I could get within this changing I,	91
If it could be, that in this southern port	160
In emptiest furthest heaven where no stars are,	96
In iron midnights in the downland fold	184
In June time once, as I was going	214
In perfect June we reached the house to let,	207
In the black Maytime when we faced the worst	232
In the dark womb where I began	37
In the harbour, in the island, in the Spanish Seas,	9
Into this barn these horses have dragged corn	189
It is the break; the pupils are at rest,	195
It may be so; but let the unknown be.	104
It may be so with us, that in the dark,	90
It was in the year of ninety-four, in March the twentieth day,	47
'It's a sunny pleasant anchorage, is Kingdom Come,	7
It's a warm wind, the west wind, full of birds' cries;	14
It's pleasant in Holy Mary	22
Just half a century since, an old man showed	227
Kneel to the beautiful women who bear us this strange brave fruit,	52
Laugh and be merry, remember, better the world with a song,	27
Let a people reading stories full of anguish	233
Let that which is to come be as it may,	99
Let us walk round: the night is dark but fine,	169
Like bones the ruins of the cities stand,	116
Man was dark, yet he made himself light; he was weak, yet he daunted	132
Man with his burning soul	67
May destiny, allotting what befalls,	240
Men have forgotten how the dance began.	185
Midsummer night had fallen at full moon,	142
Miss Piney Tricker is a girl whose wisdom is most weighty,	130
Most beautiful, most gifted, and most wise,	224
Mother Carey? She's the mother o' the witches	8
Mumblin' under the gallows, hearin' the clank o' the chain,	28
My Father, King Epeios of the Islands,	167
My friend, my bonny friend, when we are old,	40
My soul has many an old decaying room	36
Night fell, and all night long the Dauber lay	64
Night is on the downland, on the lonely moorland,	101
No, for their names are written with the light	200
No I would not be an office-boy, in a clean and tidy sash,	44

Fyfield Books

Two millennia of essential classics

The extensive FyfieldBooks list includes

Djuna Barnes *The Book of Repulsive Women and other poems*
edited by Rebecca Loncraine

Elizabeth Barrett Browning *Selected Poems* edited by Malcolm Hicks

Charles Baudelaire *Complete Poems in French and English*
translated by Walter Martin

Thomas Lovell Beddoes *Death's Jest-Book* edited by Michael Bradshaw

Aphra Behn *Selected Poems*
edited by Malcolm Hicks

Border Ballads: A Selection
edited by James Reed

The Brontë Sisters *Selected Poems*
edited by Stevie Davies

Sir Thomas Browne *Selected Writings*
edited by Claire Preston

Lewis Carroll *Selected Poems*
edited by Keith Silver

Paul Celan *Collected Prose*
translated by Rosmarie Waldrop

Thomas Chatterton *Selected Poems*
edited by Grevel Lindop

John Clare *By Himself*
edited by Eric Robinson and David Powell

Arthur Hugh Clough *Selected Poems*
edited by Shirley Chew

Samuel Taylor Coleridge *Selected Poetry* edited by William Empson and David Pirie

Tristan Corbière *The Centenary Corbière*
in French and English
translated by Val Warner

William Cowper *Selected Poems*
edited by Nick Rhodes

Gabriele d'Annunzio *Halcyon*
translated by J.G. Nichols

John Donne *Selected Letters*
edited by P.M. Oliver

William Dunbar *Selected Poems*
edited by Harriet Harvey Wood

Anne Finch, Countess of Winchilsea
Selected Poems
edited by Denys Thompson

Ford Madox Ford *Selected Poems*
edited by Max Saunders

John Gay *Selected Poems*
edited by Marcus Walsh

Oliver Goldsmith *Selected Writings*
edited by John Lucas

Robert Herrick *Selected Poems*
edited by David Jesson-Dibley

Victor Hugo *Selected Poetry*
in French and English
translated by Steven Monte

T.E. Hulme *Selected Writings*
edited by Patrick McGuinness

Leigh Hunt *Selected Writings*
edited by David Jesson Dibley

Wyndham Lewis *Collected Poems and Plays* edited by Alan Munton

Charles Lamb *Selected Writings*
edited by J.E. Morpurgo

Lucretius *De Rerum Natura: The Poem on Nature*
translated by C.H. Sisson

John Lyly *Selected Prose and Dramatic Work*
edited by Leah Scragg

Ben Jonson *Epigrams and The Forest*
edited by Richard Dutton

Giacomo Leopardi *The Canti*
with a selection of his prose
translated by J.G. Nichols

Stéphane Mallarmé *For Anatole's Tomb*
in French and English
translated by Patrick McGuinness

Andrew Marvell *Selected Poems*
edited by Bill Hutchings

Charlotte Mew *Collected Poems and Selected Prose*
edited by Val Warner

Michelangelo *Sonnets*
translated by Elizabeth Jennings,
introduction by Michael Ayrton

William Morris *Selected Poems*
edited by Peter Faulkner

John Henry Newman *Selected Writings to 1845*
edited by Albert Radcliffe

Ovid *Amores*
translated by Tom Bishop

Fernando Pessoa *A Centenary Pessoa*
edited by Eugenio Lisboa and L.C.
Taylor, introduction by Octavio Paz

Petrarch *Canzoniere*
translated by J.G. Nichols

Edgar Allan Poe *Poems and Essays on Poetry*
edited by C.H. Sisson

Restoration Bawdy
edited by John Adlard

Rainer Maria Rilke *Sonnets to Orpheus and Letters to a Young Poet*
translated by Stephen Cohn

Christina Rossetti *Selected Poems*
edited by C.H. Sisson

Dante Gabriel Rossetti *Selected Poems and Translations*
edited by Clive Wilmer

Sir Walter Scott *Selected Poems*
edited by James Reed

Sir Philip Sidney *Selected Writings*
edited by Richard Dutton

John Skelton *Selected Poems*
edited by Gerald Hammond

Charlotte Smith *Selected Poems*
edited by Judith Willson

Henry Howard, Earl of Surrey *Selected Poems*
edited by Dennis Keene

Algernon Charles Swinburne *Selected Poems*
edited by L.M. Findlay

Arthur Symons *Selected Writings*
edited by Roger Holdsworth

William Tyndale *Selected Writings*
edited by David Daniell

Oscar Wilde *Selected Poems*
edited by Malcolm Hicks

William Wordsworth *The Earliest Poems* edited by Duncan Wu

Sir Thomas Wyatt *Selected Poems*
edited by Hardiman Scott

For more information, including a full list of Fyfield*Books* and a contents list for each title, and details of how to order the books, visit the Carcanet website at www.carcanet.co.uk or email info@caracanet.